Letters to a Samuel Generation: The Collection

Rachel Starr Thomson

LITTLE DOZEN PRESS

Letters to a Samuel Generation: The Collection

Published by Little Dozen Press
Stevensville, Ontario, Canada
http://www.littledozen.com

Copyright © 2013 by Rachel Starr Thomson
Visit the author at www.rachelstarrthomson.com

Cover design by Mercy Hope
Copyright 2013

Unless otherwise noted, Scripture quotations are taken from the King James Version of the Bible.

Excerpts from the works of Amy Carmichael are used by permission of Dohnavur Fellowship.

All rights reserved. No part of this publication may be reproduced, stored in a retrieval system, or transmitted, to any form or by any means, electronic, mechanical, photocopying, recording, or otherwise, without the prior written permission of the author.

ISBN: 978-1-927658-16-1

Table of Contents

Introduction
The Collection. 1
A Christmas Letter 2
Light in the Cell 5
Daughters of Zion 6
Lights 9
I Heard The Bells On Christmas Day 12
Thoughts On Unity 14
Mrs. God 17
Miracles 18
Homecoming 22
Not In Vain 25
Training For Service. 28
Valiant For The Truth. 29
Blessing 34
Make Me Thy Fuel 37
One Body. 38
The Fourth Letter of Brother Lawrence 42
Now We Are Free. 46
In Sleep 51
Joy To The World 53
Reflections On Doing The Will Of God 56
Something To Think About. 59

Boldness	60
Seeds	64
A Question of Security	65
Allegiance	73
A Pure Work	77
Refuge of Lies	78
Not My Will	81
Molten Gods	87
A Writer's Reflections	88
Life to Me	91
Amazing Grace	92
Circumstances	98
Tyrants and Conquerors	100
Hope	104
For This Is the Will of God	105
For the Ills That Might Have Been...	110
Beauty	111
Beautiful	116
Tinsel and Trappings and the Meaning of Life	118
O Come, O Come, Emmanuel	122
The Face of Love	125
Collected Thoughts on Love	131
Voices	134
Consider the Ravens	137
Commonplace	140
Light of the World, Salt of the Earth	141
Threefold Love	149
A Dance With Mystery	151
No Scar?	155
Why Can't We Sing?	158

Bondage 162
Love Touches 163
Confession of the Sisters of the Common Life . . 167
Home 169
Second Thoughts 171
A Samuel Generation 173
Kingdoms of Light... 178
In the Morning 179
Credo 182
The Holy Mystery 185
A Great Light 189

Our Father: Excerpt from *Heart to Heart: Meeting With God in the Lord's Prayer*

Introduction

When I was seventeen and bent on changing the world, I decided to start a youth organization. I called it Samuel Generation International. We were going to be a holy generation, riding with Jesus to the ends of the earth.

Well. I learned very quickly that the world didn't need another youth organization. It didn't need me to change it, either. What it did need was more of Jesus, and the way it was going to see more of Him was if we as Christians loved Him more—knew Him better—believed and trusted in Him with all our hearts. And that would only happen as He revealed Himself.

He was doing that work of revelation in me, and I realized that I could share it. It was Christmas, the year 2000, and I sat down and tentatively began to write a reflection on God's heart in sending Christ to us. I copied it into my email, hit "send," and started on an amazing journey.

For the next four years I continued to write articles which I hoped would glorify Jesus and encourage His people, whom I loved, and still love, very deeply. Readers passed my "Letters" along, and soon they were going to mission stations and Native American reserves, pastors and homeschooling moms and dads, teenagers and elderly saints on four different continents.

That humbles me, and is not a credit to me at all.

The truth is that God's people really do love Him, and I've had the privilege to share in and encourage that love from a young age. This collection reflects not only my heart's cry, but yours as well: that we would love Him more deeply, know Him more truly, and worship Him more freely.

Though these letters owe much (including their name) to the prophet Samuel, that heart's cry was perhaps best expressed by the young man he anointed as king.

> "My soul longeth, yea, even fainteth for the courts of the Lord: my heart and my flesh crieth out for the living God. Yea, the sparrow hath found an house, and the swallow a nest for herself, where she may lay her young, even thine altars, O Lord of hosts, my King, and my God...
>
> "I had rather be a doorkeeper in the house of my God, than to dwell in the tents of wickedness. For the Lord God is a sun and shield: the Lord will give grace and glory: no good thing will he withhold from them that walk uprightly. O Lord of hosts, blessed is the man that trusteth in thee."
>
> DAVID, PSALM 84:2-3, 10-12

May God bless you as you read, and draw you closer to Himself.

The Collection

"I know that most of you who read
this are very familiar with the topics herein,
but I hope that it will do you good to be reminded
of them. So often my eyes and thoughts wander
away from the gospel into strange and weary
lands, and I am always grateful when God
brings me back to the beginning of things:
back to His Son, His sacrifice, and His grace."

from the October 2002 issue of
Letters to a Samuel Generation

A Christmas Letter

Almighty God, I don't understand. What are You doing in a child's body? Why are You putting Yourself in a dirty stable on a cold night? Why are You entrusting Your beautiful Son to the care of two confused and vulnerable human beings?

The angels are singing tonight: the King has come! The Mighty God, the Everlasting Father, the Prince of Peace: tonight He's become human. For so many long years, so many centuries gone by, we've seen snatches of His glory. The burning fire on Mount Sinai. The still small voice coming to Elijah. The waters that drowned an old world; the great cloud descending on the tabernacle; they are equal pictures of the God we serve.

Somehow, this Child doesn't quite fit. Our God is a God of power, of glory, of might. He is beautiful and frightening. An "untame lion" and a great eagle beneath whose wings we take refuge. He is a wind parting the Red Sea and a captain calling Elijah home in a flaming chariot. He is a Judge raining fire on Sodom and Gomorrah and an Angel wrestling with Jacob in the night. All of that I can understand. Beautiful and frightening; awesome and incomprehensible.

But a baby? The picture of everything that is humble and helpless. Everything I didn't think God was.

What is He doing in a manger? Why is the Glorious God of Jacob condescending to be worshiped by shepherds rather than kings; to be sought out by star-gazing strangers rather than adoring countrymen? Why is the Messiah, our Redeemer, the God of the Whole Earth, lying in a heap of straw surrounded by animals and people too busy to care?

I remember reading in Exodus when Moses asked God to show him His glory. It was all that Moses wanted. God agreed; He would let His servant see Him. But Moses could not look on God's face. All He could be given was a fleeting glimpse of the Lord moving off into the night. To come any closer to the Ancient of Days would be to invite death. Man could not stand before God in such a way.

There was a day that he could. In the garden of Eden, before sin and a serpent ever entered the world, man walked with God every day. That day is gone. Moses desired nothing more than to see God's face, but it was not a favour that could be given him. And yet, God desired to give it! The Lord Almighty wanted His children back. He wanted to walk with men again, to look on their faces and have them look on His. Yet, it was impossible for men to become pure enough to see God.

So God became one of us. The Creator of the Universe made the ultimate sacrifice. The Son of God became the Son of Man. He came into a body of dust so that He could join in our laughter and tears, in our cares and joys, as He had not done since the garden.

O shepherds, do you understand that you are seeing what Moses could not? O fishermen, do you realize that you are hearing what every generation of prophets would have given their lives to hear? Mary, Joseph, do you have any idea who you are raising? Anna and Simeon, Zacharias and Elizabeth; you who have waited all your lives for the Messiah, do you truly know what you are witnessing?

World, do you understand that the God of Judgment and Wrath has made Himself such that no one could possibly fear to come near Him? Our God, who is a consuming fire, has made Himself such that little children can play with Him and kiss Him and love Him.

Beautiful and frightening. Perhaps that little baby in the straw is more beautiful and frightening than anything we have seen yet.

The angels are singing, the prophets are rejoicing, a voice is calling in the wilderness. Somewhere, a tree is growing that will be made into a cross someday. Somewhere, a palm tree is preparing to give its fronds as instruments of worship for a king riding a donkey. Somewhere, someone is reading in Isaiah about a coming Messiah... and somewhere, a temple veil is getting ready to be forever torn. God has come down to meet us, to love us, and to be one of us.

I can't say I understand everything that has happened. I just know that the world will never be the same again.

Light in the Cell

"And a light shined in the cell"
And there was not any wall,
And there was no dark at all,
Only Thou, Immanuel.

Light of Love shined in the cell,
Turned to gold the iron bars
Opened windows to the stars
Peace stood there as sentinel.

Dearest Lord, how can it be
That Thou art so kind to me?
Love is shining in my cell,
Jesus, my Immanuel.

Amy Carmichael, from *Toward Jerusalem*

Daughters of Zion

This is dedicated to all my little sisters, natural and spiritual, and to those older sisters who are little to Someone.

Dear ones, hear these words. This is my burden for every little sister in the family of God, for all who are struggling to gain their footing in a world of shifting sands; who are so close to realizing that their refuge is under the covert of His wings, in Him who is "the rock that is higher than I."[1] He sees the time spent in front of the mirror, time spent criticizing and covering up. He knows the questions you ask, the pride and insecurity you indulge in, the vanity that tugs at you. But underneath He sees a heart beating, a heart which He desires to fill with beauty until it glows in your eyes and laughs in your smile, until your soul weeps when He does and sings when He rejoices.

He knows the pain you try to hide. He has heard the whispered words that slapped you in the face, seen the betrayal of friends, and the little foxes that gnaw at

---

1 Psalm 61:2

your soul. He knows the dark secrets, the overcoming loneliness, the pain of nights spent crying into your pillow until you shake the bed, hoping no one can hear. And He is there; He is crying too. The sins committed against you were committed against Him. He shares your rejection and knows every tear intimately. The rain outside the window on so many nights is the grief of heaven coming down for you; the thunder declares His anger. Yet in all this His purpose stands; His love will win the battle. You are a masterpiece in the hands of a great Painter. The shades of black and grey, the shadows and dark places, must be painted so that the end result will have depth and meaning.

He knows, too, the gifts and talents inside you. He knows the joy of your personality and the greatness of your dreams. Oh child, God is the ultimate dream-spinner. The rainbow threads you surrender to Him will be woven into a tapestry you could not have imagined. But they must be given up; they must be laid down at His feet to do with as He pleases.

He is your beauty-maker, your tear-bearer, your dream-weaver. He is the mother heart that will never forsake you. He is the hearth fire to keep you warm, though storms rage outside. He will take you by the hand and teach you how to dance, when the music is sad and when it is joyful.

Someday He may walk with you down an aisle and give you into the hand of a chosen man. Someday He may witness with you things you always wished to see. Surely He will suffer with you; surely He will laugh with you. Some nights He will sing you to sleep, and some nights you will dance.

In you He is creating a lady, and in you He is creating a light. And one day He will claim you as His bride, and you will step over a new horizon and into a brand new world.

"Sing, O daughter of Zion; shout, O Israel; be glad and rejoice with all thy heart, O daughter of Jerusalem. The Lord thy God in the midst of thee is mighty; he will save, he will rejoice over thee with joy; he will rest in his love, he will joy over thee with singing."[1]

---

1   Zephaniah 3:14,17

Lights

Darkness is a wearying thing.

We can only stumble around in it for so long before our eyes begin to weaken from the strain of trying to see, our feet grow tired of fighting to keep a steady foothold, our spirits are cast down for the lack of anything beautiful or good.

For many long years, there was nothing but darkness. Here and there a glimmer came through—in a fire on a mountain called Sinai, in the songs of a shepherd boy named David, and in the hearts of those who sought for something more than constant fog and darkness.

To a man called Isaiah came the word: "The people that walked in darkness have seen a great light: they that dwell in the land of the shadow of death, upon them hath the light shined.

"For unto us a child is born, unto us a son is given: and the government shall be upon his shoulder: and his name shall be called Wonderful, Counsellor, The mighty God, The everlasting Father, The Prince of Peace."[1]

And so light came. It came in the form of a child, who grew to be a man who never lost His child's heart. Light radiated from Him in the form of love that would

---

1 Isaiah 9:2, 6

not surrender to the forces of evil that buffeted Him. It came in the form of a soul so pure it was never once tainted by the stain of wrong motives or hidden pride.

Those who loved light ran to Him. But not one left His presence without having been in some way wounded, because light will not leave one corner of darkness untouched; and we all have some black thing we would like to keep safely tucked under our coats, right next to our hearts, where nothing is allowed to touch it.

Some, having seen the light, took their precious blackness and cradled it close to themselves, whispering soothingly to it as they walked away. Others gave it to the Light-Bearer to be annihilated. Thus did the woman at the well, who exulted, "He told me everything I ever did!" So did Peter, as he wept after finally seeing what cowardice was in his own heart, and surrendered even his failure to God.

Christmas is a celebration full of light. Lights on the tree and on the telephone poles downtown, lights reflecting off the waterfront and glowing through windows. In our churches we light Advent candles and sing songs about goodness and grace.

This year the Christmas Child lives in the hearts of many. Many others are facing, like Mary, the implications of having the Son of God born in them.

Jesus no longer walks the earth as a human being, but He lives and works in many such creatures. The hands that do His work are human hands, the feet that walk His paths are human feet. But it is the same now as it has ever been: those who choose darkness will eventually meet their death in one of its pits; and those who choose light will be forever on a great journey toward purity, toward good, toward eternal Christmas.

It's not always easy to be a light. People do not like to have their secret sins touched. You don't always have to preach to expose things; sometimes just the fact of your being will bring conviction to others. And so it's not your words that will be rejected, but your being.

Even so, it's not always easy to walk in light. Sometimes the darkness looks better to us. Darkness gives us our privacy; it allows us direct our own paths, even if those paths inevitably end in snares.

When we're walking in light we give up our right to darkness. We have no more right to be offended or angry; no more right to judge; no more right to live our own lives without thought to others.

Don't forget, darkness is wearying. Privacy gets lonely. Anger becomes a bitter taste in our mouth. Living our own life becomes empty and pointless.

This isn't a very Christmas-y message; there's no tinsel or holly in it. But light is, ultimately, what Christmas is about. Not one of us got to be there when Christ first took a breath of our air. But if we walk in the light, we will witness the miracle of Christmas again and again—in our own hearts, and in the hearts of those we touch.

The choice, of course, belongs to you. Will you slip quietly off into the darkness, content to live half in and half out of light?

Or will you take another step on the High Road, the way of the Father of Lights?

One more step toward eternal Christmas.

I Heard The Bells On Christmas Day

This little-known carol was written during the Civil War, America's bloodiest conflict. As brother killed brother and the horror dragged on, peace on earth seemed to be a hopeless dream. This year, some of us may feel the same way. But the promise of the Prince of Peace still stands.

I heard the bells on Christmas day
Their old familiar carols play
And mild and sweet the words repeat,
Of peace on earth, good will to men.

I thought how as the day had come,
The belfries of all Christendom
Had roll'd along th' unbroken song
Of peace on earth, good will to men.

And in despair I bow'd my head:
"There is no peace on earth," I said,
"For hate is strong, and mocks the song
Of peace on earth, good will to men."

Then pealed the bells more loud and deep:
"God is not dead, nor doth He sleep;
The wrong shall fail, the right prevail,

With peace on earth, good will to men."

'Til ringing, singing on its way,
The world revolved from night to day,
A voice, a chime, a chant sublime,
Of peace on earth, good will to men!

Henry Wadsworth Longfellow

Thoughts On Unity

Very few of the prayers of Jesus are recorded in the Bible. The longest of them is found in John 17, and takes up all twenty-six verses of that chapter. It seems to me that this address from Son to Father ought to be of immense importance to us. As it was important enough for Jesus to say it and significant enough for John to record it, we really should give it some attention. This is especially true since the prayer is one of intercession, and we are the subject of it. Yet, surprisingly little is ever said about it these days.

Here is a portion of that prayer:

"Neither pray I for these alone, but for them also which shall believe on me through their word;

"That they all may be one; as thou, Father, art in me, and I in thee, that they also may be one in us: that the world may believe that thou hast sent me.

"And the glory which thou gavest me I have given them; that they may be one, even as we are one.

"I in them, and thou in me, that they may be made perfect in one; and that the world may know that thou hast sent me, and hast loved them, as thou hast loved me."[1]

This may well have been one of the last prayers John ever heard Jesus pray, for in the very next chapter, the story of Judas's betrayal begins. At the very end of Jesus' ministry and life on earth, He found Himself concerned about our future—specifically, that we would be united.

I can't help thinking that He must be heartbroken by the attitudes of His people these days, and throughout history. Driving down Main Street in Anytown, U.S.A., you will find a Presbyterian Church on one corner, a Baptist Church two blocks away (with a separate Hispanic congregation which meets in the building after the English service—two congregations, and ne'er the twain shall meet), and an Assembly of God to finish the collection.

The community around them is being torn apart by loneliness, suicide, drugs, etc.; but the church can't do anything about it. Each congregation is too busy keeping their members away from the other denomination down the road. Each zealously guards its own territory, pouring their energy into putting up walls between church people. On the mission field, many of the same things happen.

Is it any wonder that the lost do not see in Christianity an answer to their needs? Jesus said that when Christians would unite with each other and God, then the world would believe. Through our unity, the glory and love of God operates. Without it, our light is darkened. The world will never change because they read our books, listen to our radio programs, or admire our personalities. Rather, it is the miracle of a people, one

---

[1] John 17:20-23

in heart and mind, caring for and loving each other, that will bring people to believe.

This unity of which I speak is not a mystical, mysterious experience. It is practical, hands-on. Christ loved people by healing them, feeding them, listening to them and discipling them. This kind of Spirit-inspired, down-to-earth love is that which binds together in unity. It's what He wants for us.

And it's not really that hard to achieve. In order to bring the scattered, splintered Body of Christ together again, you and I must roll up our sleeves and get to work. The question is, are you willing?

Are you willing to give of your finances to a brother who needs it?

To pray with the Charismatic, or the Mennonite, or the Anglican?

To call the lonely sister you don't really enjoy talking to, because she needs the ear and her needs matter?

To vacate the judgment seat and love a brother you think is wrong?

To learn to say "Praise the Lord" in Spanish, dance with Jewish believers, or be the only white singer in an all-black choir?

If you are, prepare for a whole new outlook on life. There's something about unity that brings love, joy, peace and glory flooding in in a whole new way.

The heart of Jesus grieves over our brokenness as a body. Will we lay aside our prejudice, our pride, and our hard-nosed inflexibility so that His heart may be blessed?

Mrs. God

Last week one of my co-workers told me about some English homework her six-year-old daughter was doing. She had to take a word and write a sentence around it. The first word was "father."

"I'm going to write, 'God is my father,'" the little girl said. "Because He is!"

Her mother nodded proudly. "That's right."

The next word on the list was "mother."

"Can I write, 'Mrs. God is my mother'?" the little girl asked.

When her mom had finished laughing over that one, she explained that there is no Mrs. God.

"There isn't?" the little girl asked. "God must be lonely!"

I went home and told Dad about the conversation, which I had found very funny indeed. Dad smiled, laughed, and then said, "Actually, there is sort of a Mrs. God."

Hmm. Interesting how, when we get rid of the higher sounding language that usually surrounds our concepts of the church—Bride of Christ, etc., and cut to the chase, we can really come up with something to think about.

Miracles

I was born into a Christian home, and so many of the words of Jesus are familiar to me. They're so familiar, in fact, that I often forget to listen to them. There's a great temptation to take for granted that which is most precious, only because God has blessed us with an abundance of it. Perhaps this is true for you, too.

I can quote many of Jesus' words in my sleep. "I am the way, the truth, and the life." "For God so loved the world that he gave his only begotten son." "I have come that ye might have life, and that ye might have it more abundantly."[1]

But recently I was reading a portion of the Bible, and I stumbled across some words of Jesus that were not written in red. I did not expect them to be there, and they took me by surprise. They are in a prophecy, in the Book of Isaiah:

"Behold, I and the children whom the LORD hath given me are for signs and for wonders in Israel from the LORD of hosts, which dwelleth in mount Zion."[2]

In that one verse I gained a whole new perspective of what exactly God is doing with us. When we

---

1 John 14:6, 3:16, 10:10
2 Isaiah 8:18

think of signs and wonders, we tend to think of flashy miracles and supernatural phenomena—"fire from heaven" sorts of things. We talk about the miracles that Jesus did as being signs and wonders, and we overlook something very important. Jesus Himself was the real sign. Jesus was the real wonder.

I've heard a lot recently about how God is moving around the world to confirm His word through signs and wonders. Christians are seeing the sick healed, the demon possessed delivered, and even the dead raised. All of this is true, and we ought to give glory to God for it. But let us not forget that our lives, our daily walks, are the real signs and wonders to the world around us.

In the book God's Smuggler, Brother Andrew talks about working in a candy factory where he and a young Christian woman endured the mockery and contempt of a large staff of worldly, foul-mouthed young ladies. Together, the two Christians did their utmost to show love and respect to their co-workers. They prayed for them, talked kindly to them, and refused to lash out in anger. The result? One of the leaders among the factory workers was converted, and one by one the workers came to Christ. They started meeting together to pray and study the Bible, and in a place that had once been a haven of vanity, the praises of God began to ring out.

Nothing supernatural happened here, if what you're looking for is something scientifically inexplicable. Yet, the greatest miracle of all did take place—lives were changed. The sign and wonder that brought about the change was the patience and forgiveness of two young Christians.

You may not think that your efforts to serve God in

the little things matter, but they do. God will see to it that your faithfulness is used for His glory. He calls us to serve Him in everything we do, cheerfully, with our whole hearts. This is not only for our benefit, but also so the world around us may understand that we have something they do not. Our attitudes, our words, and our actions, are for a sign and a wonder to those we interact with.

Not one of the apostles decided to follow Jesus because He did a miracle for them. They followed Him because He called, and in His life they saw a chance for something more. He was pure, and loving, and zealous for God in a way that they had never known. The chance to be with Him was a chance for a new life.

God does use miracles and supernatural happenings to bring people to Him, but He is more likely to draw someone through what they see in your life. If what people see when they look at you gives them hope, then they will seek the reason that you are the way you are.

Whatever trials you may be facing, remember that they are not for you alone—the way you come through them will speak volumes to those watching.

Is your marriage on shaky ground? Stand on God's word, and don't give up hope—you are for a sign and a wonder to a broken world around you. Are your children in rebellion? Stand on the word of God. Pray. Stay faithful to the call of God on your life. You are for a sign and for a wonder in a world that has given up hope.

Teenagers, are you tempted to rebel against your parents and follow the crowd? You, too, are for a sign and a wonder. Don't cripple the rest of your generation by making their mistakes with them and taking away their only glimpse of something better. You are for a sign and a wonder to them, to show them a higher road.

Finally, are you living in a second-choice life, entangled in the consequences of bad choices made in the past? No one is in a better position then you are to show the world that they need not die where they have fallen. Cry out to God, and He will lift you up, higher than you could ever have thought possible. You, maybe more than anyone else, are for a sign and for a wonder to the house of Israel.

It is not easy to be a sign, because it means that you must be constantly under God's hand—to be changed, chastised, and purified. But every step of the way will be worth it. Every part of the journey, though you go through fire and water and back through again, will yield a reward.

Do not expect everyone to understand. When the Holy Spirit came down on Pentecost, people accused the disciples of being drunk. When Jesus cast out demons, the Pharisees claimed that He did so by the prince of demons. When the Son of God bowed His head on the cross and died, onlookers laughed. Many were blind, and they could not see what was happening in front of them.

But some did. Some opened their eyes. And today, some are looking for a new life.

"Behold, I and the children whom the Lord hath given me are for signs and for wonders in Israel from the Lord of hosts, which dwelleth in mount Zion."

Homecoming

Crowds are lining the streets of heaven, every heart beating the same thought: "He's coming home!"

The saints and the angels have been watching since the beginning of the Lord's strange journey. They wept for Him, were angry for Him, and rejoiced with Him. Most of all, they missed Him.

A hush falls over the crowd as the gates of Heaven open, and suddenly He is there. He looks on them all, and smiles. In a moment a shout of victory swells from the ranks, as Jesus walks among them once more. He pauses here and there to look into a certain face and catch a sparkling eye. Gabriel smiles as he meets his Master's eyes. It was his joy to herald the king's arrival on Earth, but his joy is far greater now, when he can welcome Him home.

Michael, the mighty Archangel, salutes as Jesus passes by him. How many times did he hold back his legions from going to the Lord's rescue? Many times his heart burned with anger against the Father of Lies, and again and again he was forced to hold back. The day is coming, Michael knows, when he will no longer hold back. It will be his joy and his crown.

Here and there an angel bows his head, face flushed with pleasure at the Master's smile. These came to Jesus in the wilderness and in Gethsemane; His ministers when no one else cared. They could not do much. There were times they wanted to move mountains for their Lord—but now He is home again, and what they could not do no longer matters.

And now Jesus has passed by the ranks of angels on His walk down the main street of Heaven, and He looks on the saints. Abraham, Moses, David: there are tears in their eyes. For the first time Jesus stands before them not just as a God, but as a man. They are humbled and overwhelmed.

At last the strange entrance is over, and Jesus is seated at the right hand of His Father. It is good to be home at last. It is good to be in the city where love reigns. Yet, in His eyes is a far away look. He has left a part of Himself behind, willingly so. In going home, He does not mean to leave His followers alone.

The welcome in the eyes of the saints and angels—on Earth its closest match was the welcome in Mary's eyes when she saw her first son, and the awe and love showed by Anna and Simeon in the Temple.

The allegiance that the angels silently give—was it ever matched on Earth? John the Baptist gave everything to prepare Jesus' way, yet he doubted. Peter swore his undying devotion many times, but he denied the Lord. The love and loyalty that are the heartbeat of Heaven exist only in traces and shadows on the earth. But Jesus' heart is not here. He has given everything to His people on the earth. He has come back to the City of Light in order to prepare a home for His followers.

This day is a day of rejoicing for Heaven, a day of uncertainty for the small group of Christians that now live in the all-too earthly Jerusalem. The saints and angels have their Lord with them again, the disciples have only a fervent hope to cling to and the promise of a coming Comforter.

But Jesus knows what is ahead. This Kingdom of love and light is soon to be born on Earth, in the hearts of men. This welcome is for them, too. They are being brought into a new life, into a new day. They don't realize it yet, but someday it will all become clear.

Life for Jesus' followers isn't going to be easy, but ease was never in the plan. And when their pilgrimage is over, they too have a home waiting for them. They have a City of Light and Love, where legions of angels and saints gone before wait to greet them.

Someday they will all hear the greatest words that could ever be spoken to a human soul:

"Welcome home."

"Let not your heart be troubled: ye believe in God, believe also in me. In my Father's house are many mansions: if it were not so, I would have told you. I go to prepare a place for you. And if I go and prepare a place for you, I will come again, and receive you unto myself; that where I am, there you may be also.

"I will not leave you comfortless: I will come to you. Yet a little while, and the world seeth me no more; but ye see me: because I live, ye shall live also. At that day ye shall know that I am in my Father, and ye in me, and I in you."

John 14:1-3, 14:18-20

Not In Vain

It is the ultimate question of life. The one question we find ourselves asking again and again, no matter who we are or where we come from. The heart of our nation asked it as we watched the Twin Towers fall on our television screens. We ask it when the job we wanted so badly slips away from us, we ask it when we lose a loved one, we ask it in loss and sometimes in blessing. It is the burning, searing question of life: "Why?"

Sometimes the answer comes. More often, our only answer is the ash-filled breeze that tells us something has happened, something is gone, and we do not understand.

As I write this, my family is facing a situation in which we are left holding ashes. For a period of time we have poured our lives into something, only to lose it. And we don't understand why.

Weeks ago, the Lord began to prepare me for this. He began to speak to my heart, to tell me that He knows how we feel. He has felt the same way.

"Don't be ridiculous," you're saying. "God knows everything. Jesus is God. He has never felt like this. He has never wasted His time, wasted His life for nothing."

In Isaiah 49:4, Jesus speaks words I never thought I'd hear Him say: "Then I said, I have laboured in vain, I have spent my strength for nought, and in vain; yet surely my judgment is with the Lord, and my work with my God."

Have you ever beat your fists against the doors of Heaven, demanding to know what God was doing? If you have, perhaps all you gleaned from the experience were bloody knuckles. You see, God doesn't always tell us exactly why things are. He only asks us to trust Him, to believe that our work truly is with Him.

Jesus, hanging on a cross, looked out over a dark world and saw the end of His life approaching fast. And what had become of His work of three years? The disciples had denied Him and fled. Rather than glorifying God, the people of Israel were mocking and spitting on Him. For one brief moment, I believe the emotions of the Son of Man cried out for understanding. Yes, He knew that God was in control. Absolutely He understood what He was doing. He knew the reasons. But the cry came, anyway.

"My God, my God, why hast thou forsaken me?"[1]

And there was no answer.

Three days later, Jesus stepped out of the tomb. The answer to Jesus' dying prayer had come. In His death, Jesus handed all of His earthly ministry over to the Father. He trusted Him to be faithful with it. And just as the Resurrection proved that nothing had been in vain, so, in your life, God knows exactly what He is doing. You can trust Him with your work, with your prayers, with your efforts, and even with your mistakes. No

---

1   Mark 15:34

matter what the circumstances say, God is still faithful.

It is not in vain. True, you cannot see the reasons now. Maybe you will never see the reasons in this life. Only believe what God has said. Your judgment is with the Lord, your work is with your God—and He does not let anything slip through the cracks.

All of you missionaries who have spent your lives on the field, giving your all for people who so often do not want to hear, who so often take advantage of you while turning a deaf ear to your message: your work is not in vain. God has seen your sacrifice, and He has accepted it.

Mothers on your knees for rebellious children, who pray and weep for all the prodigals who have wandered in one sense or another—I know that sometimes it seems that God is not listening. I know that it seems you have poured your entire life into your children for nothing. Just remember that it is just this point that Jesus reached on the cross, as He watched all of His children scatter. And never, never forget what happened when Friday ended forever and Sunday finally came.

To everyone who has ever followed the call of God and found that it led to disappointment, persecution, and pain: your work is with your God. Your judgment is with the Lord. And He is faithful.

Offer all you do as a sacrifice to our God, the Eternal, the Almighty, the Great I Am. In His hands, nothing is ever for nothing. Nothing is ever in vain.

Training For Service

> "The best training is to learn to accept everything as it comes, as from Him whom our soul loves. The tests are always unexpected things, not great things that can be written up, but the common little rubs of life, silly little nothings, things you are ashamed of minding one scrap. Yet they can knock a strong man over and lay him very low."
>
> Amy Carmichael, from *Candles in the Dark*

Valiant For The Truth

The other night I sat down for a rare evening of television, and I was struck by an appalling fact: despite society's preoccupation with violence and power, we are a nation of wimps.

I did not arrive at this through watching the actual shows. Rather, I went for the real mirror of society—the commercials. Do they ever tell a story! Does your head hurt? Take Advil. Do your allergies bother you? Take something for it. Do you have arthritis? Pop a pill! Osteoporosis? Take a pain-killer. Constipation? We've got something for that, too!

Mind you, I am not against pain-killers for pain-killers' sake. However, I do find them rather indicative of a society in which personal comfort is the goal set before us for which to strive. We live in a nation where dreams for the future usually involve red convertibles, tropical vacations, and air conditioning. Nothing in life, the ads seem to say, has the right to make you uncomfortable.

I understand that physical discomfort is no fun, and perhaps I am unfair to label us wimps because we refuse to let anything hurt. However, I'm afraid that this preoccupation with making life comfortable is only an outward manifestation of a much deeper problem inside. In our spiritual lives, it seems, we have sacrificed truth on the altar of self. We have chosen to ignore everything that makes us uncomfortable, everything that would drive us to change, in order to live a life of ease and security.

Our public schools and universities preach the gospel of tolerance. Truth is what you want it to be. Don't you dare suggest that anyone else's lifestyle could be wrong—after all, right and wrong are relative terms, aren't they? Those who take a stand become targets. It's a little ironic, actually. We're so tolerant that we'll gun down anyone who disagrees with us—anyone who insinuates that there might be such a thing as absolute truth in this world.

Our disregard for truth shines through in every aspect of our culture. In the movies and on TV, we applaud the clever rather than the righteous. Modern heroes lie their way through situations instead of fighting their way through. Even our view of ancient heroes says something about how much we love truth. Robin Hood, the thief, is admired and loved; while Sir Galahad, the pure knight of the Round Table, is typically snickered at.

Thousands of years ago, the prophet Jeremiah spoke God's words to a similar society, one which was about to be taken into captivity in Babylon. All around him, false prophets stood up in the name of the LORD and told the people of Israel that they would be just fine. They were God's chosen people, weren't they? They had nothing to worry about. The false prophets of Jeremiah's day were preaching peace, where there was no peace. They stood on the brink of disaster and prophesied that God would bless His people no matter what they did.

And then there was Jeremiah, the lone voice of sanity and righteousness in a corrupt world. Casting all concern for his own life on God, he had the audacity to tell the truth. He was persecuted and maligned for it. His reputation was trashed. He was hated and mocked. The most tragic thing of all was that Israel, confronted with truth, would not listen to it. They, like us, were more concerned with their own comfort and peace of mind than they were with reality. As the guillotine came sweeping down on their necks, they closed their eyes and willed themselves into a state of apathy and unbelief. They would not hear the truth. Jeremiah 9:3 vividly describes the Israel of that day—and, at the same time, paints a terribly accurate description of our own world:

"And they bend their tongues like their bow for lies: but they are not valiant for the truth upon the earth; for they proceed from evil to evil, and they know not me, saith the Lord."

We are desperately in need of a generation that will stand up and be valiant for the truth. It is easy to blame the state of society on the media, on Hollywood, or on the educational elite. But this is only another form of avoiding the truth. Our prevalent attitude of wishy-washiness toward truth, like all sins, begins in our hearts. Truth hurts. It hurts our pride. It hurts our self-image. So we run from it, or do our best to justify ourselves.

We may not like it, but truth tears down before it ever starts building up. When God called Jeremiah, he said, "See, I have this day set thee over the nations and over the kingdoms, to root out, and to pull down, and to destroy, and to throw down, to build, and to plant."[1]

Yes, this ancient truth-teller was called to build and to plant. But first, the words of God that flowed through him would root out, would pull down, destroy, and throw down the works of darkness. For those of us who are harbouring works of darkness in our lives, this is not a pleasant thought.

Our Lord Jesus Christ is the Truth, personified. In order to follow Him, there is a decision to be made. Remember? "Take up your cross and follow me. Go, and sin no more." He has called us out of darkness. Those who would follow Him soon find that many things in their lives have to be rooted up before anything good can begin to grow. The word of God can't really bring forth fruit in our lives while we are allowing weeds to choke it out.

"Valiant for the truth." I want these words to describe me. My first instinct, of course, is to take what I believe to be true and start bashing people over the head with it. If I can tear down all the sin in everybody else's lives, then I can pretty much put off dealing with my own heart. It's a good thing for me that Christ does not allow me this luxury. You see, His brand of truth is a humbling thing. It doesn't judge and condemn others. His brand of truth took Him all the way to the cross, while ours so often wants to crucify everyone else.

"Judge not," He says, "that ye be not judged. For with what judgment ye judge, ye shall be judged: and with what measure ye mete, it shall be measured to you again. And why beholdest thou the mote that is in thy brother's eye, but considerest not the beam that is

---

[1] Jeremiah 1:10

in thine own eye? Or how wilt thou say to thy brother, Let me pull out the mote out of thine eye; and, behold, a beam is in thine own eye? Thou hypocrite, first cast out the beam out of thine own eye; and then shalt thou see clearly to cast out the mote out of thy brother's eye."[1]

Then there is the other end of the spectrum, that of making inoffensiveness our ultimate goal. This is the gospel of tolerance. We refuse to take a stand for anything, and so, as the saying goes, we'll fall for anything. Jesus didn't operate on this kind of "truth," either. He knew that people are not saved by being coddled. If we become professional yes-men, all we'll manage to do is cripple those we ought to be helping.

This world, this Church, this generation desperately needs men and women who will be valiant for the truth! We need men and women who will deal with God on an intimate level, allowing Him into every dark corner of their lives, so that truth can reign triumphant in them. We need men and women who can stand up for what is true without condemning others; who can call sin "sin" and do it in the Spirit of Christ. On our own accord we are capable of tearing up and leaving only rubble. With the Spirit of God leading us, the rubble becomes fertile ground in which the Kingdom of God can grow.

It begins with us. It begins in the deepest part of our hearts. Will we become another Israel, led away into captivity because of our own willful blindness? Or will we become "valiant for the truth upon the earth"?

In this world of over-drugged, under-developed human beings, it's about time that a few heroes stand up. How about you?

---

1   Matthew 7:1-5

Blessing

Have you been to the movies lately?
Have you spent any time with teenagers?
Have you listened to the tone of the media?

If so, you may have noticed an alarming trend. Society believes, knowingly or not, that family is "uncool."

Youth leaders tell teens that their parents are out of touch, so they should come to their pastor if they have problems. Older siblings spend oodles of energy trying to ditch their younger sisters and brothers in order to spend time at the mall, the movies, the bowling alley—anywhere where there are friends and no family.

Reunions, birthday celebrations, and Christmas get-togethers are seen as annoying obligations. No amount of heartwarming, shallow movies about love and family seem to be able to offset the damage of this general slide away from family ties.

In church we hear about how curses are passed through the generations; at the therapist's we hear about how parents have permanently scarred their children and doomed them to life in and out of prisons, marriages, and happiness. This is probably true. But it is one side of the picture.

As a product of the other side, I would like to protest.

Oh, my family has problems. We're human. But let me tell you about the blessings that have come through the generations.

When I was a little child, I had aunts and uncles around me constantly. I grew up feeling protected and loved. I didn't have to have anyone's constant attention. Just knowing they were there was security. About six years ago, my family moved away from our home in Canada and went to California, and I lost that shelter. Three months ago, I moved back home. A week ago I went to a cousin's thirteenth birthday party, and most of the aunts and uncles were there. Once again, I felt that shelter.

Every day, my paternal grandparents take a walk and pray for each of their grandchildren by name. Every day at evening devotions, my maternal grandparents ask the Lord to draw their children and grandchildren to Him. My walk with the Lord has been blessed in many unusual ways. And I don't have to wonder why.

My mother, grandmothers, and aunts have taught me about being a woman, and more especially a lady. My uncles open doors for me. Uncle Stephen took me on my first date when I turned sixteen. Dad would take me out for coffee and ask about my needs and my interests every so often, just checking up on me. My cousins have taught me to lighten up and have fun, and to love people no matter what. My sisters and brothers have taught me to look for the good in people even when the bad is glaringly obvious. And when I've found the good, it's been beautifully, brilliantly, wonderful.

In my mother's Mennonite family tree, there are martyrs for Christ. In my father's Scottish history, there are preachers, pastors, and Sunday School teachers. For generations, there is prayer.

I have ten siblings to teach me about teamwork and growing up, eight aunts to giggle and trade stories with, four grandparents to show me what true priorities should be, six uncles to treat me like a princess, over forty cousins to laugh with, love with, and live with, and two parents to train me up in the way I should go.

I am a product of generational blessings and generational grace. Have there been problems passed down? Yes. But I believe the good things outweigh the problems.

To every one out there who thinks family isn't cool: please, please, start building new relationships with those God has given you. Serve your sisters and brothers. Love your nieces and nephews. Pray for your children and grandchildren. It isn't ever too late to start.

Make Me Thy Fuel

From prayer that asks that I may be
Sheltered from winds that beat on Thee,
From fearing when I should aspire,
From faltering when I should climb higher,
From silken self, O Captain, free
Thy soldier who would follow Thee.

From subtle love of softening things,
From easy choices, weakenings,
Not thus are spirits fortified,
Not this way went the Crucified,
From all that dims Thy Calvary,
O Lamb of God, deliver me.

Give me the love that leads the way,
The faith that nothing can dismay,
The hope no disappointments tire,
The passion that will burn like fire,
Let me not sink to be a clod:
Make my Thy fuel, Flame of God.

Amy Carmichael, *Toward Jerusalem*

One Body

Imagine, for a moment, the following scenario.

A hand and a mouth have gotten together over lunch to "fellowship." Somewhere in the conversation, talk turns to a common acquaintance—a foot, to be exact.

"Did you see Foot last week?" Hand asks. "He was down in the mud, trudging alongside the rest of the world."

"Hmm," Mouth hums in agreement. "I was witnessing at the time."

"I was praising the Lord. Poor Foot seems to have his priorities messed up."

"He would find life a lot more fulfilling if he'd spent less time in the mud and more time telling people about Jesus."

"Praise the Lord we've got our priorities straight. Ministry comes first." Hand thinks for a moment. "Hey, do you know what Eye was looking at yesterday?"

Meanwhile, Foot and Eye find it hard to throw themselves into their work of trudging and looking. After all, some rather more exalted members of the body seem to think there's not much purpose in mud and surroundings. Still, Foot and Eye don't have much choice about their work—but, since it doesn't do any good overall, why bother working at it?

Of course, this creates some problems. Foot doesn't bother to go many places, so Mouth doesn't get much chance to witness to new people. Eye doesn't see needs, so Hand can't meet them. And so on.

The Apostle Paul writes about this very thing in I Corinthians 12:15-22.

"If the foot shall say, Because I am not the hand, I am not of the body; is it therefore not of the body? And if the ear shall say, Because I am not the eye, I am not of the body; is it therefore not of the body? If the whole body were an eye, where were the hearing? If the whole were hearing, where were the smelling?

"But now hath God set the members every one of them in the body, as it hath pleased him. And if they were all one member, where were the body? But now are they many members, but yet one body. And the eye cannot say unto the hand, I have no need of thee: nor again the head to the feet, I have no need of you. Nay, much more those members of the body, which seem to be feeble, are necessary."

I've often noticed (and been guilty of) a strange phenomenon among Christians. We have got it into our heads that some professions are infinitely more valuable than others. An evangelist is worth more to the Kingdom than a carpenter, for example. Or a missionary does more for God than a grandmother.

The Bible has a completely different criteria for workers in the Kingdom of God than that which we seem to live by: "And whatsoever ye do, do it heartily, as to the Lord, and not unto men; Knowing that of the Lord ye shall receive the reward of the inheritance: for ye serve the Lord Christ."[1]

Whatsoever ye do. Be it babysitting, preaching, mothering, rocket science—whatsoever ye do, do it heartily as unto the Lord. We are commanded all through the scripture to be faithful in that which God gives us to do.

How many Christians resign themselves to the fact that they are not called to the mission field—meaning Africa, or Indonesia, or some such far-off place—and completely miss the mission field that God has already placed them in? We admire those Christians who are full time servants of God, without realizing that we share their position. In whatever we do, we are the servants of the Lord Christ.

Perhaps we classify "ministry" as something someone else does as a way of avoiding responsibility. Anyone with some talent can preach a sermon, but who dares live one? We can all "do" church every Sunday, but are we willing to live as the Body of Christ all the rest of the week?

On the other side of the fence, many in ministry seem to be using the "lower" callings of others to give themselves an ego boost. Instead of humbling ourselves before the Lord and allowing Him to lift us up, are we guilty of exalting ourselves before men? Does our pride get its weekly fix by trampling other Christians down?

How much are we, in our thoughts, words, and actions, crippling the Body of Christ? These are the people that Christ gave His life for. Every brother or sister in the Lord is a temple of the Holy Spirit, whether they

---

[1] Colossions 3:23-24

work at a gas station or a mission station.

"For I say, through the grace given unto me, to every man that is among you, not to think of himself more highly than he ought to think, but to think soberly; according as God hath dealt to every man the measure of faith.
"For as we have many members in one body, and all members have not the same office: So we, being many, are one body in Christ, and every one members one of another."

Romans 12:3-5

The Fourth Letter of Brother Lawrence

" My dear sister in the Lord,

"I sympathize with your difficult situation. I think that freeing yourself of your present responsibilities for a while and devoting yourself entirely to prayer would be the best thing you could do for yourself. God does not ask much of us. But remembering Him, praising Him, asking for His grace, offering Him your troubles, or thanking Him for what He has given you will console you all the time. During your meals or during any daily duty, lift your heart up to Him, because even the least little remembrance will please Him. You don't have to pray out loud; He's nearer than you can imagine.

"It isn't necessary that we stay in church in order to remain in God's presence. We can make our heart a chapel where we can go anytime to talk to God privately. These conversations can be so loving and gentle, and anyone can have them.

"So why not begin? He may be waiting for us to take the first step. Because we have such a short time to live, we should spend our remaining time with God. Even suffering will be easier when we are with Him, but without Him, even the greatest pleasures will be joyless. May He be blessed in everything!

"Gradually train yourself to show your love for Him by asking for His grace. Offer your heart to Him at every moment. Don't restrict your love of Him with rules or special devotions. Go out in faith, with love and humility.

"I remain your servant in the Lord."

from *Practicing the Presence of God*, by Brother Lawrence

notes from the author
DECEMBER 2002

My dear friends,

I have never cried over an ezine before. I cried over this one.

I typed it instead of writing it out by hand, so there are no tear-stains on a page to remind me of what I felt when I wrote it. But perhaps you can see the tear-stains in my words.

Ecclesiastes 7:3 says, "Sorrow is better than laughter: for by the sadness of the countenance the heart is made better." It's true. Sorrow deepens joy, in a very strange sort of paradox. And one day sorrow will no longer work its deepening effect, as it gives way to joy:

"When the Lord turned again the captivity of Zion, we were like them that dream. Then was our mouth filled with laughter, and our tongue with singing: then said they among the heathen, The Lord hath done great things for them.

"The Lord hath done great things for us, whereof we are glad. Turn again our captivity, O Lord, as the streams in the south.

"They that sow in tears shall reap in joy.

"He that goeth forth and weepeth, bearing precious seed, shall doubtless come again with rejoicing, bringing his sheaves with him."[1]

I am not the only one who is suffering this Christmas, I know that very well. Perhaps you all have your own private griefs to bear. So I invite you: sorrow with me, and I pray that your heart will be made better for it. I look forward to the day when we will all laugh together.

In Jesus' great love,
Rachel

---

[1] Psalm 126

Now We Are Free

It is 8:04 pm., three days before Christmas. I am writing now because something very important has just happened.

My grandmother is free.

Before the clock struck eight tonight, her heart stopped beating. She has gone away from us.

It was not so long ago that she told me what she most looked forward to. "Do you know what the best thing about heaven is going to be?" she asked me. "It's not that I'll be with my loved ones again... though that will be wonderful. It's not the streets of gold or the angels or anything else like that... it's *Him. It will be so wonderful to see Him. To be with Him. To talk with Him. Can you imagine it?*"

Yes, Grandma, I can imagine it... but I know that my imagination does not begin to describe what you are feeling now. Since you were seventeen you have lived in His service. His truth has lit your way. His love has filled your heart and flowed over to touch my life, and the lives of so many. So many.

And now you see Him.

I don't know what the obituary will say. "Lois Thomson died at the age of seventy-three, in the city of Windsor, Ontario, where she spent the last forty-some years of her life. She leaves behind a mother, a sister, a husband, eight children, seven children-in-law, and forty-seven grandchildren. She will be sorely missed."

True enough, but it doesn't begin to say what must be said. It doesn't say what the angels are saying, but their words have an echo in my own heart.

Lois Thomson went to the place of her heart's desire today.

She has long seen through a glass, darkly, but now she sees clearly.

She was sown in corruption; she is raised incorruptible.

Praise Him.

She was sown in dishonour; she is raised in glory.

Give praise to the Lord of Life.

She was sown in weakness; she is raised in power.

Praise Him, for His mercy endureth forever.

Her mortality is swallowed up in life! Death is swallowed up in victory!

O death, where is thy sting? O grave, where is thy victory?

God has at last become her all in all.

She has gone into the holy of holies, and she need never come back into the dirt and darkness of this world again.

Truly, she is free.

My grandmother was a remarkable woman. Her life touched more people than can be counted. She wasn't perfect. Of course not. She was human just like you and me. And she was beginning to tire of life. Oh, she still had a lot to live for, but it wasn't easy anymore. She was often tired and discouraged. I am crying as I write this, but I am grieving for myself, not for her.

How can I?

She has answered the call of her beloved.

"The voice of my beloved! behold, he cometh leaping upon the mountains, skipping upon the hills. My beloved is like a roe or a young hart: behold, he standeth behind our wall, he looketh forth at the windows, shewing himself through the lattice.

"My beloved spake, and said unto me, Rise up, my love, my fair one, and come away. For, lo, the winter is past, the rain is over and gone; The flowers appear on the earth; the time of the singing of birds is come, and the voice of the turtle dove is heard in our land;

"The fig tree putteth forth her green figs, and the vines with the tender grape give a good smell. Arise, my love, my fair one, and come away.

"O my dove, that art in the clefts of the rock, in the secret places of the stairs, let me see thy countenance, let me hear thy voice; for sweet is thy voice, and thy countenance is comely.

"Take us the foxes, the little foxes, that spoil the vines: for our vines have tender grapes.

"My beloved is mine, and I am his: he feedeth among the lilies. Until the day break, and the shadows flee away, turn, my beloved, and be thou like a roe or a young hart upon the mountains."[1]

This world was not cruel to my grandmother. She had many people to love her, and the light of God shone in her life. But a deeper longing was within her still, and she did not fear death because of it. She knew there was more to come for her.

C.S. Lewis once wrote these words: "Creatures

---
1 Song of Solomon 2:8-17

are not born with desires unless satisfaction for those desires exists. A baby feels hunger: well, there is such a thing as food. A duckling wants to swim: well, there is such a thing as water... If I find in myself a desire which no experience in this world can satisfy, the most probable explanation is that I was made for another world."

Why should I mourn for this one whom I love? She is leaping and skipping upon the mountains. She has found the desire of her heart. She has discovered the meaning of the words, "It is finished."

Some might say that it's a terrible thing to lose a loved one just before Christmas, but I am glad it happened now. It brings the miracle of Christmas all the closer. Some two thousand years ago, a man was born who gave hope substance and made faith worth having. The Son of God took a human name, lived a human life, and died a human death. Why?

So that my grandma could be free today. And so that I could cry and still write these words. He rose from the dead so that we could, too. Without Jesus, all hope is vain and all joy is empty. But because He lived, died, and lives again, every one of us can look death in the face and say, "I do not fear you. Nor can you truly take anything away from me. Everything I have is hidden in Him who does not die."

My grandmother has gone to be with him, which means that she is not so very far away from me. He is as close as a prayer, as close as the air that hangs around me. That is why love transcends death, because we can't ever be really separated. He has seen to that.

This Christmas, my grandmother's thoughts and words and eyes are full of *Him*, only Him. I pray that all of those who read these words would also fill their souls with *Him*, with His nearness and His love. As Grandma lay dying this past week, a prayer continually filled my heart: "Father, glorify Thy name." He has.

I love you, Grandma. Thank you for teaching me this one last lesson.

My dear friend Janet says that for Christians, there is no such thing as good-bye, only see you later. So.

I'll see you later.

In Sleep

He gives to His beloved in sleep,
For when the spirit drifts from fields of time,
And wanders free in worlds remote, sublime,
    It meets Him there,
    The only Alone Fair.
    But were it bidden to tell
    The heavenly words that fell,
Dropping like sunlit rain through quiet air,
It could not, though it heard them everywhere.

Were some small fish in a rock-pool close confined,
Swept in the backwash of a wave to sea,
Could it describe that blue immensity?
    Could the caged bird,
    Whose happy ear had heard
    The lark sing high in heaven,
    And had escaped, be bidden
To bind that rapture fast in earthly words?
Not so is bound the song of singing birds.

Nor can I tell what He gave me in sleep—
The mind, still conscious of the body's stress,
Hindered awhile, and in a wilderness

    I walked alone,
    Till One a long time known
    Drew near; 'Lord, may I come?
    For I would fain go Home.'
'Not yet, My child,' then waves on waves of blue,
Like the blue sea, or air that light pours through.

This is not much to bring of that land's gold,
But one word lingers of the shining dream,
'Be comforted, all ye who by a stream,
    Watch wistfully,
    Lest your beloved be
    Swept to some shore unknown,
    All desolate, alone;
It is not so, but now as heretofore,
The Risen Christ is standing on the shore.'

- written by the missionary Amy Carmichael during the last years of her life, when she was confined to her bed in constant pain because of an accident. It was included in her book, *Toward Jerusalem*.

Joy To The World

Joy to the world!
The Lord is come. The desire of every nation, every true heart, has come. The King is here. The Messiah. The One who will never let you down. As much as you have been hurt, so He will heal. As much as you have become disillusioned, so He will fulfill all your beliefs. As much as you have run dry, He will fill you up—with His love. Oh, His love!

There He is, a dirty little child in a dirty little manger; and that young girl is his mother. He can't sleep because the sheep are making too much noise, but it's all right. He'll sleep later. Tonight is not a night to sleep, anyway.

The King has come.

See Him grow. See how the people love Him, how everywhere He goes He commands respect. His following begins to form, a band of devoted ones begins to gather around Him. They are not great men, not mighty warriors or deep philosophers. Mostly they are fishermen, and tax collectors, and very common men. It is good that their King was born in a manger, or they might not dare follow Him.

Now look... do you see how the world begins to hate Him? It is because He obeys and loves His Father so much. He loves too much for a world of hatred.

They react the only way they can. They loathe Him. They taunt Him. They plot against Him.

But here and there someone sees Him for who He is. John the Baptist sees, as the Holy Spirit descends from heaven before his wide eyes and remains on this young cousin of his. Mary of Bethany knows. That's why she sits at His feet, content to let the world fall apart around her.

The woman with the alabaster box knows. Do you see what she has done? She has wept on his feet, anointed Him with perfume, dried His feet with her hair. He describes her actions best: "She has done what she could."[1] May we all do the same.

Peter and John and James know. They were there when the veil was stripped back from their eyes and they saw Him as He really was, shining with the brilliance of all the stars and talking with the Law and the Prophets, Moses and Elijah.

Why has He come? Because there is a gap between God and man, and it must be closed. The disciples come to Him and ask, "Lord, teach us to pray." And He says, "Begin this way: Our Father who art in heaven, hallowed by Thy name."[2] In the past the prophets and kings prayed to the King of Heaven. They prayed to the Lord of Hosts, to the Creator of the Universe. They prayed to the God above all gods. But now a new thing comes: "Call Him Father," Jesus says. Abba. Father. Daddy. This is why He came.

And now watch and see His death. See it in all of its horror. This is the night the world went mad. They mock, they spit, they murder without thought for what

[1] Mark 14:8
[2] Matthew 6:9

they do. For three terrible, horrible days, light is extinguished in darkness.

But not forever. He is risen! He has come back to us. It is true what He said:

"Verily, verily, I say unto you, That ye shall weep and lament, but the world shall rejoice: and ye shall be sorrowful, but your sorrow shall be turned into joy.

"A woman when she is in travail hath sorrow, because her hour is come: but as soon as she is delivered of the child, she remembereth no more the anguish, for joy that a man is born into the world.

"And ye now therefore have sorrow: but I will see you again, and your heart shall rejoice, and your joy no man taketh from you."[1]

Joy to the world.

The Lord is come!

---

1 John 16:20-22

Reflections On Doing The Will Of God

I was sitting and reading my Bible one day, when a scripture jumped out of nowhere and hit me. You know what I mean. You're sitting on the couch in front of the big living room windows, soaking up the late morning sun. Your mind is half on, half off what you're reading, when a previously unassuming little verse stands up and calls for attention.

The verse in question is in Hebrews. It's quoting one of the prophets quoting Jesus, and it says, "Then said I, Lo, I come (In the volume of the book it is written of me,) to do thy will, O God."[1]

There was something strong about that statement, something that made me sit up straighter. I pictured Jesus, desert sun at His back, striding into Galilee with purpose thundering in every footstep. Here He comes, face set like flint, joy and grimness both in His heart: walking into destiny.

Something about it made my heart leap. The spirit of the verse called to mind another scripture: "For ye shall go out with joy, and be led forth with peace: the mountains and the hills shall break forth before you into singing; and all the trees of the field shall clap their

---

1   Hebrews 10:7

hands."[1]

As a teacher I am gratified when the children respond to my commands and suggestions with enthusiasm. Their faces light up, they cheer and smile, and run to do the thing they are asked.

This happens often. But just as often, a child will complain, pout, and drag his feet when it comes to obedience. Sure, they'll obey—but I can't make them like it. On these occasions, I still love the children, but I'm not particularly pleased with them.

When God had made it clear to me that I was supposed to leave my family and move to Michigan, I had more than one night in which I fell into speculation and self-pity.

"But I'll be lonely there."

"What if I can't work in ministry anymore?"

"What if the environment weakens my faith?"

"I'll have to get up early in the mornings. I hate getting up early."

I was spiritually dragging my feet, and I knew it. Oh, I meant to be obedient. But be joyful about it? Well, that was a whole 'nuther ballgame. On one of my pouty nights, that verse in Hebrews suddenly sprang to mind. The difference between my attitude and that

---

[1] Isaiah 55:12

of Jesus shamed me. The will of God in His life was that He suffer and die, and yet He embraced it wholeheartedly.

In the Lord's prayer we read, "Thy will be done on earth as it is in heaven." In heaven there is no foot-dragging; no moping and muttering over the perceived disadvantages of disobedience. I deeply believe that this world will begin to change when Christians learn to embrace the will of God in their lives.

"Thy will be done in me, as it is in heaven."

"Lo, I come, do thy will, O God."

Something To Think About

Much of our modern prayer
has no power in it because there is no
heart in it. We rush into God's presence,
run through a string of petitions, jump
up and go out. If someone should ask us
an hour afterward for what we prayed,
oftentimes we could not tell. If we put so
little heart into our prayers, we cannot
expect God to put much heart into
answering them."

R.A. Torrey, from *How to Pray*.

Boldness

This morning I sat in an adult Sunday School class where we watched a video about the death of Jesus, and then began to talk about the impact of His life. It was, said the teacher, a life that was like a stone dropped in the middle of history, creating a ripple effect that spread all over the world. The question was presented to us: how can we, as a church, live lives that will cause a similiar ripple effect? How can we bring the Kingdom of God to the world in a way that will cause a stir and affect the world around us?

We broke up into discussion groups, and attempted to come up with some good answers in the space of fifteen-twenty minutes. At the end of this "brainstorming session," representatives from various groups stood up and shared some of their ideas.

Some said we ought to pray more. Others said that we ought to "use the power of God" more. But overridingly, every group had one answer: what we lack, they said, is boldness. Boldness in the workplace. Boldness on the street. We should confront sin openly, stand up for what we believe in. It is boldness that will create the needed ripple effect and change the world around us.

As I sat and listened to my brothers and sisters

sharing this particular point, I couldn't help feeling that we were missing the mark somehow. The more I thought about it, the more I realized why. For most of us, the word "boldness" is synonymous with the word "outspoken." And the truth is that words are worthless. Without a living, vibrant foundation behind them, words are nothing more than a plastic sword that will melt as soon as a little heat is applied.

St. Francis of Assisi made an oft-quoted comment many years ago: "Preach the gospel at all times. When necessary, use words." In our modern Christian society, the idea of reaching the lost usually conjures up images of a style of evangelism that focuses on street preaching, handing out tracts, and accosting everyone we meet with the words, "Are you saved?" True, these methods have proved effective in the past. They have their place, under the direction of the Holy Spirit. But if we will honestly look at the teaching and examples of Jesus and the New Testament writers, I believe we will find that the Lord and His followers mostly agreed with St. Francis.

For instance, most of us have an idea that Jesus spent most of His time sitting on hilltops preaching at people. The truth is, this was not the focus of His ministry at all. Yes, He did teach—when people asked Him to. Most of His teaching to the masses came in direct response to a question or a circumstance that naturally led to teaching. Even when He did teach, His meanings were often cloaked in mysterious parables that only the true seekers were able to grasp.

If we want to follow the example of Jesus, I think we'll find that bold words are not the key at all. Instead, it is a boldness in our way of life that will create a ripple effect, and touch the world around us. People came to Jesus and asked Him questions about the Father because His life was a powerful demonstration of that Father. His actions spoke a thousand times louder than His words. "I have a greater witness than John's," Jesus said. "For the works which the Father has given Me to finish—the very works that I do—bear witness of Me, that the Father has sent Me."[1]

If we are to follow the example of Jesus, then it is our lives—not just our mouths—that should point the way to the Father. I don't mean that we should all go out and start healing people, raising the dead, and turning water into wine. God has not necessarily given us all the power to do those things, right now. God has not called us to try and work miracles in our own power, but to imitate the character of Jesus' life. The power to work miracles is a gift that God gives to His children, and perhaps we will all see miracles done through our hands. But God knows that most of us would use this power to draw people to ourselves, if we had it now. Before we can be given the power to be strong, we must receive the power to be weak—to live lives of humility, honesty, and obedience. The boldness we are called to seek does not lead to a flashy lifestyle or a soapbox mentality. Rather, we are called to seek a life of bold servanthood, quiet faith, and love.

Jesus did not say that His people would be known by their outspokenness, or by their carefully crafted methods of evangelism and their slick church services. Rather, He said, "By this shall all men know that ye are my disciples, if ye have love one to another."[2]

Paul spoke of the emptiness of words without love in I Corinthians 13:1—"Though If I speak with the tongues of men and of angels, but do not have love,

[1] John 5:36
[2] John 13:35

I have become a noisy gong or a clanging cymbal" (NASV).

I believe that a boldness of life is created through love. As we make love for God the primary focus of our life, the ripple effect will come to pass. As we love Him, we will desire to obey Him. A desire for obedience leads to a life of prayer, for it is largely in prayer that we come to see the steps of obedience it is necessary for us to take, and receive the power to take them. Prayer, as a constant act of communion with God, begins a change in our lives that opens the door for God's love to flow through us to others, saved and unsaved alike. And therein is the ripple effect created. Miracles begin to happen, as faith works by love and brings the Kingdom of God into our lives.

Yes, we do need boldness in our lives. Boldness of obedience. Boldness of faith. Boldness of love. Rather than creating methods for evangelism and beating ourselves up because we aren't outspoken enough, perhaps we ought to be focusing anew on our personal relationship with our Father. We need to live our lives as Jesus did, making love for our Father the primary reason for life. Everything else in His life flowed naturally out of the communion of Father and Son. And so it can be, in our lives. As we love Him boldly, we too will begin to know His love for all the world, and as we demonstrate that love, the needy around us will respond.

When love is the hallmark of our lives, people will begin to ask questions. And then, finally, we can talk. People will listen.

Our lives will have given meaning to our words.

Seeds...

"I introduced the concert by saying that God is on the side of those who are weak, persecuted, and vulnerable—one of the many truths of God which Christians and Jews hold in common. We share this idea that God reaches out to us in love and blessing, that He is our Redeemer as well as our Creator, that He made us in His own image to love Him and serve Him, and without this relationship we're like seeds lying outside the soil: full of potential but not of growth."

Adrian Snell, musician, from *Children of Exile*.

A Question of Security

I can remember it very clearly. Laying in bed in the dark, cool hours of the morning, listening to a clock tick away the minutes and wishing that my wide eyes would go to sleep already. I remember staring up at the planks of the high, wooden ceiling and watching the desert breeze rustle the curtains.

Mostly I remember the questions running through my head.

What if? What if this happens... what if that?

Only a few days before, I had heard from the Lord, telling me to leave home and go to teach school in Michigan. Not a very scary prospect, really, but for me it was a little nerve-racking. I'd never lived away from home. I'd never taught school. The thing worrying me most was the prospect of leaving the ministry I'd been involved with and going to a place where I knew the spiritual climate was not going to be so intense. A place where there would be a lot of dangers, spiritually speaking.

What if?

This same stomach-churning worry had come around to bother me at various times throughout my life. When I was younger, I couldn't call someone on the phone without feeling sick. I'm not sure what I was afraid of, but I was. The first day of school felt the same way. So did going to youth group in California, right after my family moved west. They were little things, but they all set off the same little warning bells in my head. Something here is not safe.

Safety and security are terribly important to us as human beings. I can't remember being born, but I imagine a baby is asking the same question as it enters the world: is this safe?

God built this instinct for safety into us for a reason. After all, if we didn't have it, we might have run ourselves off of the face of the earth a long time ago, jumping off cliffs because, well, it looked like fun at the time.

At the same time, God gave us the will to deny that instinct for safety. He built other desires into us as well—desires for freedom, for growth, for new horizons. And that's a good thing, because He very rarely allows us to live in safety for long. It takes a crazy sort of courage to follow in the steps of the Lord; the same sort of courage it takes for a soldier to go into battle. Even if that soldier is guaranteed victory in the end, as we Christians are, there are no promises that the journey to the end will be a smooth one.

Take the pioneer missionaries of ages past for an example. When Gladys Aylward began saving her shillings for a train ride to China, she was not thinking in terms of security. If she had asked God if it would be safe or not, the answer would have to have been no. The tiny Englishwoman knew she would be facing hunger, cold, exhaustion and hostility as she attempted to preach the gospel in a far northern province of

China. She did not expect to face the guns and terror of Japanese soldiers as World War II spread its influence even to her remote corner of the world. Faced with some of life's hardest decisions, the missionary became a spy, a relief worker, and a mother to more than 200 orphans. Today, her legacy of courage and faithfulness to God is an inspiration to thousands of people, not to mention the descendants of those who first heard the gospel from her lips. Was it worthwhile for her to follow the call of God? Yes. Was it safe? Well, no, not exactly.

Is it dangerous to follow the Lord's leading? Oh, yes. But we must ask ourselves—is safety what we truly ought to seek? Did God send us into this world to build walls around ourselves, or to go out and face the enemy? Most of us, in theory, would agree with the second statement. So why, when the marching orders come, is it so hard for us to step out on faith?

For me, the answer came clearly that sleepless summer night. I wrestled with my questions until the realization finally hit me that God would be in Michigan, too. What then was I really worried about? I realized that night that I was putting my faith in the wrong thing—in circumstances, instead of in the Living God.

Therein lies our problem, I think. We measure safety by circumstances, instead of seeking it under the Shadow of His Wings—the only place we are truly safe.

In the book of Jeremiah, the long-suffering prophet records a story that graphically illustrates this same principle. At the time the story takes place, most of the Jewish people had been removed from their homeland and taken into captivity in Babylon. The population of Judah was now made up of a few farmers and poverty-stricken people who were not judged any kind of threat to the Babylonians. An Israelite named Gedaliah was appointed to govern them.

Before long, refugees from the captivity began to straggle back into Judah from their hiding places in Moab, Ammon, Edom, and all of the surrounding countries. Included among them were soldiers who had been hiding in the fields, including a man named Johanan. Gedaliah was a good ruler, and the people of Israel slowly began to pick up the shattered pieces of their lives.

One day, Johanan approached Gedaliah with a rumour: that one of the soldiers, Ishmael the son of Nethaniah, had been enlisted by the king of Ammon to assassinate the governor. Johanan offered to kill Ishmael first, but Gedaliah, believing that the rumour was false, refused to allow it.

Secure in his belief that Ishmael meant him no harm, Gedaliah and a number of other Israelites sat down to a friendly meal with the son of Nethaniah. When the time of fellowship was over, the treacherous Ishmael killed Gedaliah and all of the men that were with him. He and his fellows kidnapped a good number of Israelites and headed for Ammon.

It didn't take the story long to reach the ears of Johanan, who rounded up a band of men and headed out after Ishmael. In a battle in the valley of Gibeon, Johanan rescued Ishmael's captives and killed most of his men, although Ishmael himself escaped into the wilderness, eventually making it back to the land of the Ammonites.

All of this made the Jews realize just how precarious their position in their burned-out land was. There were very few of them, and their appointed governor, who had kept their conquerors happy, was dead. Their enemies, men like the king of Ammon, were on every side.

Frightened and shaken by Ammon's nearly successful attempt to destroy them, the remnant of Israel approached the prophet Jeremiah with a request. "Inquire unto your God for us," Johanan asked, "and we will do whatever he says."

Jeremiah returned to them with the word of the Lord: "Be not afraid of the king of Babylon, of whom ye are afraid; be not afraid of him, saith the Lord: for I am with you to save you, and to deliver you from his hand. And I will shew mercies unto you, that he may have mercy upon you, and cause you to return to your own land. But if ye say, We will not dwell in this land, neither obey the voice of the Lord your God, saying, No; but we will go into the land of Egypt, where we shall see no war, nor hear the sound of the trumpet, nor have hunger of bread; and there will we dwell: and now therefore hear the word of the Lord, ye remnant of Judah; Thus saith the Lord of hosts, the God of Israel; if ye wholly set your faces to enter into Egypt, and go to sojourn there; then it shall come to pass, that the sword which ye feared, shall overtake you there in the land of Egypt, and the famine, whereof ye were afraid, shall follow close after you there in Egypt; and there ye shall die."[1]

It was a pronouncement that was hard for Johanan and the Israelites to accept. After all, telling them to stay in the land was a bit like telling Jews in the 20th century to stay in their ghettos while the Nazis closed

---

1   Jeremiah 42:11-16

in. The circumstances did not favour staying in Israel, certainly. Just over the border to the south, the land of Egypt beckoned.

The choice was clear: put your trust in circumstances, or put it in God and obey.

Sadly, the Israelites had not yet learned the lesson that the captivity to Babylon was meant to teach them. Johanan became angry and accused Jeremiah of speaking falsely. "God has not said this to us," they told him. "We are going to Egypt."

Jeremiah went with them; weeping all the way, I suspect. Egypt of that day had all the food and water the refugees would need, and a military to protect them. The government was friendly to them. It looked like a paradise.

Tragically, this "paradise" was nothing but a cruel mirage. For Egypt, too, was about to be judged—the sword of Babylon would fall across its pyramids just as surely as it fell on the wall of Jerusalem.

The Israelites of that day would have done well to remember the words of their father David, who, while he lived a life of dangers, tragedies, and triumphs, never forgot just where his safety lay: "My soul, wait thou only upon God: For my expectation is from him. He only is my rock and my salvation: He is my defence; I shall not be moved. In God is my salvation and my glory: the rock of my strength, and my refuge, is in my God. Trust in him at all times; ye people, Pour out your heart before him: God is a refuge for us. Selah."[1]

If God is directing your feet in a new path, you are likely to be weighing this age-old question—where is my safety, truly? The circumstances may look daunt-

---

1   Psalm 62:5-8

ing, and Egypt is just over the border, only a few steps back from obedience. Whatever the decision facing you is, remember the lesson of Jeremiah and Johanan: of trust in circumstances, or trust in God. His word is true, and He never fails.

I remind you, with David: trust in Him at all times, ye people. God is a refuge for us.

Selah.

notes from the author
MAY 2002

The difference between our struggles and those of the world is that our enemies can't be physically attacked. We seem to think that a physical enemy is necessary if we're going to fight, and so we pick someone out of the crowd and attack him. A fellow Christian is acting on behalf of Satan (it does happen) so we make him our enemy. Or we jump in with the rest of the people around us and make terrorists and evil governments our enemy. That's all right, if you're willing to follow Jesus' instructions as to how to treat human enemies. "Bless those who persecute you... if your enemy hungers, feed him, if he is naked, clothe him... love your enemy."[1]

---

1 Matthew 5:44, Romans 12:20

Allegiance

Once there was an army, a mighty band of joyful warriors who had come together under the banner of a Captain they loved. By His side they toiled and fought; through days of rain and times when the sun beat down mercilessly on their heads. But the Captain's smile and the Captain's love burned brighter than any desert sun, and all sacrifices were counted as joy by the soldiers.

One young soldier could think of no happier life than his. To him, the dirt on his face was like a crown, and every bit of work he could do for his Master was sheer joy. When he fell asleep at night, his Captain's face graced his dreams, and though he was often exhausted, he slept the sleep of the faithful.

One day, as he was out on a scouting mission, a stranger appeared. He was impressive to look at, well-groomed and not so muddy as most soldiers. As the young man worked, the stranger began to speak to him. A suggestion here, a comment there—the young man was impressed with the stranger's evident concern for his welfare. The young soldier concluded, after a while, that the stranger must have been sent by the Captain.

Every day, the stranger worked with the young soldier. Over time, the stranger's ways became more and more attractive to the young soldier. Dirt under his fingernails no longer seemed like a mark of honour, and the stranger showed him ways to work while looking out for himself, too. Ambitious dreams of personal glory tugged at the young man's heart, and his sleep became restless and troubled.

The companions who had once seemed glorious now appeared foolish and ignorant, and the young man sometimes blushed with shame at the thought of being counted among them. He began to withdraw from them, and when one day a fellow soldier made a sharp remark to him, the young soldier hid in his tent and stewed, while the stranger stroked his pride and told him what a fine fellow he really was.

One night an order came from the Captain:

"Get up and follow Me at once. We must journey through the Valley of Suffering."

The young man groaned and started, slowly, to get up. Then he heard the stranger's voice.

"He does not mean for you to go now. The Captain knows that you need your rest. Besides, the Valley is such an unpleasant place. The Captain loves you so much, He would not ask you to go through it."

The young man thought that the stranger's words rang true. The Captain did not really mean for him to go, not now. So he rolled over and went back to sleep.

So it happened, more and more. The Captain's orders came, and then the stranger's—and the young soldier's allegiance, once so strong and undivided, began to waver. Things that had been black and white turned a fuzzy shade of grey. The young man's work became shoddy and his enthusiasm half-hearted, and his fellow soldiers often suffered for his carelessness.

Then one day, the Enemy charged the camp. The Captain's orders were clear—"Stand and fight!"—but the stranger said, "Run." And the young soldier, who now knew that allegiance can only belong to one, turned and ran. An arrow from the Enemy's bow struck his back and pierced him through, and the young soldier fell dead on the ground. And the stranger, whose name was Flesh, slowly faded away.

The Christian Church today is a victim of divided allegiance.

In our society of rights and privileges, we have come to believe that we owe ourselves something. Forgetting that the call of Jesus is to lose our lives for His sake, we press on through the confusing muck of a battle in which two opposing captains give orders.

Recently my family and I have been fighting a difficult battle. Throughout, some of the hardest fights have been connected to that other captain, Flesh. Words were spoken to us that hurt, and Jesus said, "Forgive them, love them, and continue to be faithful."

Immediately, Flesh stood up and told me to be offended. "Forgive in word, but put up a divider between you and them. Hint to people about what a martyr you are. Cause people to take sides, and work for your 'enemy's' destruction and humiliation." There was a choice to be made, between the cross of Christ and the feather bed of self-indulgence.

My dad often says that the opposite of love is not hate, but selfishness. The Bible makes it clear that as Christians, we have a responsibility to deny the flesh in every situation, and follow the Lord who loves us.

Christian have no personal rights. We are owned by Christ, who bought us with His own blood, and so it is His right to defend us, justify us, provide for and uplift us—not ours.

The Flesh is a tempting master. He offers comfort and self-satisfaction, and likes to pretend that he is making you more fit to serve the King. He seems to inspire, though in truth he is a coward and a manipulator. He dreams of glory, yet he creates only shells of men; whitewashed tombs full of dead men's bones. His whispers are enticing and deceptive, for "There is a way that seemeth right unto a man, but the end thereof are the ways of death."[1]

But the real Master, the True Captain—nothing can be compared with His service! The Flesh tells you that you are beautiful—the Master's smile, reflected in your face, makes this so. The Flesh promises false happiness—the King exudes joy like the flowers produce perfume.

The Flesh wants to lift you high, but it's a precarious platform, because the King is down in the mud. He is working alongside His children. And when the day comes that He is exalted before all men, He will take His own with Him. In the heat of the battle, when the Flesh says that you are weak and useless, the Captain says, "My strength is made perfect in weakness."

When the going gets tough, we will listen to the voice whose commands we are accustomed to obeying. Fences cannot be sat on for long, and true allegiance is never really divided.

Whose commands are you listening to?

---

1   Proverbs 16:25

A Pure Work

Don't be surprised if there is an attack on your work, on you who are called to do it, on your innermost nature—the hidden man of the heart. It must be so. The great thing is not to be surprised, not to count it strange—for that plays into the hand of enemy.

"Is it possible that anyone should set himself to exalt our beloved Lord and not become instantly a target for many arrows? The very fact that your work depends utterly on Him and can't be done for a moment without Him calls for a very close walk and a constant communion of spirit. This alone is enough to account for anything the enemy can do.

"But there are limits set. Greater is He. I have just read that glorious word in Romans 5, 'They that receive the abundance of grace... reign in life, through the One, even Jesus Christ.' And this was written to slaves in Nero's wicked palace. What daring of faith the Spirit gave to Paul.

"It costs to have a pure work. Not for nothing is our God called a Consuming Fire."

Amy Carmichael, from *Candles in the Dark*

Refuge of Lies

I remember trying to hold a conversation with someone and being constantly frustrated in my attempts to reach her, because the real "her" was hiding. She was looking out at me through a smiling, stylized mask—while the real person was bleeding and dying inside.

I've known people with two faces, or more than two—one righteous, one gentle, one vicious and sarcastic. One face was more pleasant than another, but all buried the real person, choking for air under a heavy cloak of falsehood. We live in a world of fake smiles, fake laughter, fake worship, and fake tears. And it's no wonder, for the god of this world is a liar, and the father of it.[1]

In the beginning, Adam and Eve sinned against God. Their first instinct was to hide—to take refuge behind a lie, to pretend that everything was all right. Likewise, Cain buried his murdered brother. Get rid of the evidence. Pretend it's okay. Remember David, committing murder to cover up the truth? Or Moses, burying the Egyptian in the sand?

Hiding behind a lie.

People take shelter behind illusion for plenty of reasons. They do it because they're afraid of being hurt.

---

1   John 8:44

They're afraid of rejection. But most of all, we take cover in lies because we're afraid to face up to the truth about ourselves: that we are lost, depraved, rebellious sinners in desperate need of our God.

In our culture, we pull the cover of lies tight around us and keep our masks smiling. We murder children to cover up the consequences of our own personal sins. We write sitcoms so that we can laugh at divorce and homosexuality. We sing patriotic songs and write grandiose speeches so we can pretend that the problems of hatred and violence don't begin much closer to home: right here in the hearts of you and me.

Our lies are poison. They poison our world, our cultures, our homes, and our own souls. They harden us and deafen us, they blind our hearts to God's truth and hold us back from reaching for Him. Is it any wonder that Satan so quickly taught us to lie?

Thousands of years ago, Isaiah spoke eloquently of the tragedy of those who hide behind a refuge of illusion.

"Wherefore hear the word of the Lord, ye scornful men, that rule this people which is in Jerusalem.

"Because ye have said, We have made a covenant with death, and with hell are we at agreement; when the overflowing scourge shall pass through, it shall not come unto us: for we have made lies our refuge, and under falsehood have we hid ourselves:

"Therefore thus saith the Lord God, Behold, I lay in Zion for a foundation a stone, a tried stone, a precious corner stone, a sure foundation: he that believeth shall not make haste.

"Judgment also will I lay to the line, and righteousness to the plummet: and the hail shall sweep away the refuge of lies, and the waters shall overflow the hiding place.

"And your covenant with death shall be disannulled, and your agreement with hell shall not stand; when the overflowing scourge shall pass through, then ye shall be trodden down by it…

"For the bed is shorter than that a man can stretch himself on it: and the covering narrower than that he can wrap himself in it."[1]

As followers of Christ, we know of a better way. Jesus proclaimed that the truth would set us free! The answer to sin is not to pretend that it isn't there, but to confess it and repent of it. Repentance leads to forgiveness; and forgiveness, to freedom. Freedom to be, at last, exactly who God made us to be. Freedom to let down our masks. Freedom to come out from the shadows, away from the fig leaves. Freedom to be real, and to walk with a real God.

Why then, are so many Christians still hiding? Instead of letting Christ's image be formed in us, we are building our own image for all the world to see. The Bible calls us children of light. What are we doing in the darkness?

This Christian walk is a battle. It demands constant vigilance. We fall into lies so easily. And the fight is hard—but it is worth it. The world cannot see Christ in you if you are hiding behind a mask.

Let the mask down. Let the illusion shatter. If you are standing with Christ, nothing can destroy you. It can only make you stronger. It can only set you free.

And that, my friend, is the truth.

---

1 Isaiah 28:14-18, 20

Not My Will

They had done this before, these men of Galilee. The ritual of Passover ran through their lives like a binding thread, a constant, comforting presence in an often turbulent world. They had celebrated it many times, in exactly this way, with family, friends, and countrymen. It never changed; its message of hope in the memory of past deliverance never wavered.

But this year, something was different. There was a heaviness in the air, a foreboding that hung about their heads like a cloud. This year it seemed that the Angel of Death was drawing near to their own doors, and they could only pray that the ancient deliverance be enacted once more, in their own day. They might have tried to laugh it off, but the strange words of their Master kept echoing in their ears: "Behold, we go up to Jerusalem, and all things that are written by the prophets concerning the Son of man shall be accomplished. For he shall be delivered unto the Gentiles, and shall be mocked, and spitefully entreated, and spitted on: And they shall scourge him, and put him to death: and the third day he shall rise again."[1]

They did not understand, but they felt the grim determination rising up inside them. He would not die.

---
1 Luke 18:31-33

They would not allow it, not if they had to give their lives to prevent it.

Now, in the Passover meal, He gave them no comfort. Once again he spoke of death. So calmly He spoke! It was beyond reason that anyone should be so matter-of-fact about His own death—His own crucifixion!

"This is my body, broken for you... take, eat."[1] They ate, and their hearts grew harder against the darkness that beat against them. There would be heroes made before this night was over. They would die for Him. So Peter proclaimed, and Jesus only shook His head.

"I tell you, Peter, that the cock will not crow this day before you shall three times deny that you even know me."[2]

The Passover meal over, the disciples could not help but notice the troubled countenance of their Lord. They felt helpless; too stupid to know what to say. But they would give Him some comfort at least by staying by Him, and so they all went with Him when He withdrew to Gethsemane.

Ah, but now He wanted to be alone. He asked them to wait, and they did, but the weariness of the night folded over them and they drifted away in sleep. They were exhausted; exhausted with the confused intensity of emotion that had assailed them in the past few days.

A short way away, the Master held audience with God His Father. He was not immune to the darkness. It wore at Him as it did His disciples, tormenting Him until the blood dripped down his face. "My Father!" he cried. "Let this cup pass from me—yet not what I will.

---

[1] I Corinthians 11:24
[2] Luke 22:24

Oh Father, let thy will be done!"[1]

At last the time came, and He rose from the rock where He had prayed and went to His disciples. For a moment His face betrayed a deep tenderness as He watched them, sleeping with troubled brows. "Sleep on now," He said, "and take your rest: it is enough, the hour is come; behold, the Son of man is betrayed into the hands of sinners." They stirred in their sleep, and then came wide awake as His voice strengthened and rang out in the dark. "Rise up! let us go; lo, he that betrayeth me is at hand."[2]

Then the soldiers came, their torches tearing gashes of orange across the star-lit sky, swords glinting with the ugly light, faces twisted and sneering. And Judas stepped forward, and kissed the Master, and the betrayal was complete.

Peter knew the moment had come to prove his love and his loyalty. Now was the moment to fight, though it cost him his life. Now was the hour of courage, when adversity would bring forth her children; when trouble would prove him a hero or a knave.

And he was ready.

He leaped forward and his sword cut a determined swath through the air. There was a cry of pain, and he saw the blood flowing from the head of a servant. He raised his arm again, his eyes flashing wildly, adrenaline rushing through him like a river released from a dam.

But Jesus stopped him. He knelt and picked up the servant's severed ear, and he healed him. His eyes turned on Peter, and they were full of reproach.

---

[1] Luke 22:42
[2] Mark 14:41-42

"Peter," they seemed to say, "do not fight against the will of God."

All of the disciples heard those words in Jesus' bearing as He gave Himself into the hands of His enemies, willingly. Oh, how they wished to fight! Given their own will, they would have fought to the death for Him. Surely, that was what God would have them do!

But no. No, this was God's will. It was God's will that Judas betray the One who loved him. It was God's will that the soldiers come with strong arm and sword. It was God's will that Jesus be arrested. God's will that He die.

The truth came crashing in on them like a bone-crushing tide, and they could not stand before it. They saw in that moment the terrible will of God, and their faith failed them.

They ran.

If we can convince ourselves that God's will is all wine and roses, then we will have no trouble sticking by it. But when the will of God is terrible—what then? How many of us scatter into the night when the soldiers come? Where, then, is our faith?

On that night, when all the world went mad, one Son of Man kept faith.

They took Him away to Pilate, and Peter followed at a distance. His heart was beating wildly as he went; a million confused thoughts whirled through his brain. But he could not bring himself to give up. Not yet.

Then in the courtyard, Peter watched as his Lord was whipped, mocked, and taunted. He watched the horrible pageant acted out by the men in the courtyard: a coronation; crown of thrones pressed onto the head of Him who was truly a King. Peter watched the madness of it all. He saw the triumph of Evil over Good.

And this was the will of God. Jesus did not fight. Before the priests He gave no great vindictive speeches. He made no wild protestations. He allowed it all without complaint, for this was the will of the Father.

Jesus Christ looked straight into the terrible will of God and He did not fall. He simply bowed His head and submitted. He trusted His Father, and His trust did not waver no matter what the Father asked Him to do.

But Peter did not have that trust. Hot-blooded heroism had no place in the courts of Pilate, and so Peter fell. Three times he denied His Lord before the cock crowed.

We all know the rest of the story. We know that the madness of the world that night swept Jesus away to Golgotha. We know that in the last moments before His death, He cried out in anguish to His Father, and His Father turned His back.

But we know something else, and because we know it, the will of God can never truly be terrible again. We know that Jesus rose from the dead.

God brought the greatest Good this world has ever known out of the greatest Evil it has ever committed. Yes, His will that night was terrible, but His love was greater. Sometimes love demands sacrifices we do not understand, but we can bow our heads and know that God has not forsaken us. We need not abandon trust, faith, and hope as Peter and the other disciples did when they fled the garden that night.

In our churches we love to talk about the "wonderful plan" God has for our lives. We would rather not talk about His terrible will—the will of God that allows a September 11 to rock our country, that allowed the Holocaust, that allows thousands of Christians across the world to suffer horrific persecution. We don't understand it any more than Jesus' disciples understood Golgotha.

I realize that I am standing on dangerous ground when I refer to the above events as being "the will of God." I don't say that God takes pleasure in these things, but He does allow them; and that is a very great test of faith indeed.

But we need not fail the test. Jesus rose from the dead, after all.

My prayer is that when we, the people of God, come into our own personal Gethsemanes, we will not run from our Father's will. There is no shame in sweating blood, in crying out to God that we cannot do it without His strength. There is no shame in wishing that things could be otherwise. But let us not forget that His prayer that night ended with the words, "Not my will, but Thine, be done."

Molten Gods

It is written: "Thou shalt make thee no molten gods."

When you think of God, you should really think of him, and not of a molten god which you have made in your own image.

>from *Ten Rungs: Hasidic Sayings*, compiled and edited by Martin Buber

A Writer's Reflections

As I lately sat down to gather my scattered thoughts and write something, the thought came to me that recent issues of Letters to a Samuel Generation have been on the short side. This bothered me for a little while, as I wondered what it meant in regard to my spiritual life. Since I usually write articles based on what God is teaching me, did my lack of material indicate a dearth in my spiritual growth?

After thinking this over, I was able to say, with relief, that it did not. I am grateful to be able to say that the great Teacher continues to teach in my life as much as ever. Unfortunately, many of His lessons don't seem to translate into writing very well. If they were neat and tidy lessons, I'm sure they could be nicely formatted into a medium-sized article with a clever opening and a thought-provoking finish, along with three or four scripture references and an abundance of colourful illustrations and moving, poetic language.

Alas, the lessons of God don't fit into semantic boxes any more than the Teacher Himself does. Rather than neat and tidy, they tend to be wild and unruly, and it does not help that they often come to me in vague snatches before settling down in my mind as layers of hard sediment to anchor my life on.

Perhaps some of you can relate to what I am saying. Surely my musical friends have experienced the frustration of taking something very important to them and trying in vain to communicate it through lyrics and melody. More than one of my dear ones dances, but how does one truly express the beauty and holiness of God through a series of movements? How does a painter explore the mysteries of Creation and Creator with colour and line?

This frustration is not limited to the arts. How many of us have ever opened our mouths to try and tell someone else about the mysteries of our Lord, the Great I Am That I Am, and found that words, tears, and voice can never fully say what needs to be said?

So to all of you, my brothers and sisters, who with me live in the Light of a Lord greater than we have the power to say, let me offer a few thoughts of encouragement.

First of all, let us not give up trying to say the impossible. However you attempt to do it, don't ever stop! Press in, ever deeper; reach up, always higher. Chase your vague impressions down until they break over you with the power of a tidal wave. Memorize the scriptures that speak to you and keep thinking on them, constantly, until they overwhelm you with the strength of meaning contained in their few words.

When we've come to be so full of the wonder of God that we cannot contain it any longer, then our words, our music and our dance, our paintings and our very lives, will begin to take on some of the nature of the Spirit that is inspiring them.

Secondly, may we never become so focused on the

trivial that we forget to be grateful that our God is an I Am That I Am and not an I Am That You Want Me To Be. The mysteries of God cannot be found out by textbook. We can't learn all there is to know about Him in a few years of study, or even in a whole lifetime of consecration. No matter how deep we go, His ways are deeper. His love, His mercy, His justice, His very nature is greater than we will ever know in this life, and maybe even in the next.

And that, for a race of creatures who are constantly cutting themselves off from true life by putting the period on the end of the sentence long before they should, is infinitely good news.

Life to Me

Cause me to hear, for it is life to me;
I perish when I am away from Thee,
Love of my love,
Tell me, where walkest Thou?
I would be with Thee now.

Let me be Thy companion, even I,
For whom Thou once didst in a garden lie;
Love of my love,
Than all my dear more dear,
Tell me, may I draw near?

I may, I may. Thou callest me to come;
O Dweller in the gardens, this is home.
Love of my love,
Dear Lord, what would I more
But listen, serve, adore?

> Amy Carmichael, from *Gold Cord*

Amazing Grace

"Oh foolish Christians! Who has bewitched you that you should not obey the truth, before whose eyes Jesus Christ was clearly portrayed among you as crucified?

"This only I want to learn from you: Did you receive the Spirit by the works of the law, or by the hearing of faith?

"Are you so foolish? Having begun in the Spirit, are you now being made perfect by the flesh?"

Hard words. We can almost feel the frustration with which Paul writes; we can almost see his fist pounding the table in front of him. Yes, these are hard words—but they are also, when taken into our hearts and applied to our lives, words that impart the most incredible freedom! For those who did not recognize the above quotation, it comes from Paul's Epistle to the Galatians, Chapter 3:1-3 (with a slight modification). These words of Paul's have spoken to me many times, and I hope that they might speak to you as well. They have humbled me, saddened me, and most of all, released me, for in them is the bountiful mercy and power of God revealed.

My struggle with grace dates back a number of years. Struggle? Oh, yes, I've struggled with the grace of God. And so, I suspect, have many Christians. The Galatians certainly did. I'm not sure exactly why grace is such a difficult thing to embrace, but it is. Perhaps it is our pride that gets in the way, that wants to claim some credit for ourselves. In Ephesians, Paul says that grace is the gift of God—not of works, lest any man should boast. What God wants to give us, our blind pride would rather earn. This may be why so many people have to hit rock bottom before coming to the Lord. Sometimes, it takes the absolute decimation of pride to make us able to meet God.

It was a number of years ago, while I was working in ministry, that I slipped into a belief that God expected me to earn my way into His good favour. Some of scripture's more frightening passages tormented me, with their warnings of sheep and goats, of castaways and those who "fall from grace." My works became a matter of desperately trying to keep my head up above water, instead of flowing from my love for and faith in the Lord of life. The harder I tried to work my way into God's good books, the more aware of my own utter depravity I became. No matter how hard I prayed, studied, and worked for the Lord, I could not rise above my failings. My fellowship with God became hindered, and my work became crippled. I could hardly be effective for a God who must certainly be unhappy with me.

During all of this, I still held to the doctrine of salvation by faith through which I had come to the Lord in the first place. This other belief, this trying to perfect myself through the flesh, was a new development. At last I came to a place where I could take it no longer. I fell on my knees and cried out to God:

"Lord, I have to know what grace is, or I can't go on anymore. I can't keep serving You without this understanding."

I felt impressed to read the Book of Romans, which

I have always had difficulty in understanding. Feeling a bit as though I was being led to a dry well and told it was going to start filling up at any moment, I started reading. Every day I read a chapter and memorized a few verses in it to mull over for the day, and when I felt that I had come to an understanding of what I had read, I would move on to the next chapter.

What I learned in Romans would take a long, long time to articulate, and I'm not going to try and record it all here. Rather, I would like to tell you about the other scripture passage that God used to crystallize the concept of grace in my mind, and in my heart. It is found in John chapter 8, and to me it is one of the most moving passages in the whole book.

It is the story of grace.

In it, a woman is brought to the Great God of the Universe, embodied in a man named Jesus Christ. She is brought roughly before the Judge of the Ages, thrown down at His feet and accused as an adulteress. She is certainly guilty. She was caught in the act and brought here! She lays on the ground, her head hanging, not daring even to look at Him. This is the God whose fingers once wrote on two tablets of stone, who commanded for every person in every time that "Thou shalt not commit adultery!" This is the God who demanded the penalty of death for this crime. It is at His feet she now lies, and it is to His ears the challenge is thrown:

"Teacher, this woman was caught in the act of adultery. Now, Moses in the law commanded us that such should be stoned. But what do *You* say?"[1]

For a moment the Son of God's eyes sweep the crowd, and then He stoops down and begins to write

---

1   John 8:4-5

on the ground. There is a moment of shock. Is He ignoring them? And then He looks up, and says quietly, "He who is without sin among you—let him throw the first stone."[1]

And He is back to His writing in the dirt. A very old man with a very white beard abruptly turns and leaves the scene. Others follow, some quickly, some slowly, with more reluctance. The Christ's words have come to bear on every man. They stand all convicted; all guilty. So they leave.

And He is left.

The sinless One.

The Alpha and Omega, Judge of the Hearts of Men, the Great I Am, He who rained fire on Sodom and Gomorrah; the One before whom the angels cry, "Holy! Holy! Holy is the Lord of Hosts, the whole earth is full of His glory!"[2]

His Law has been broken by this woman. His Rule has been mocked. Almighty God stands affronted.

His voice is gentle as He asks, "Woman, where are your accusers? Has no one condemned you?"

She raises her eyes, just a glimmer of hope beginning to warm her heart. "No one, Lord."

And oh, so quietly He says words that cause the heavens to shiver, that cause all of creation to draw in its breath and gasp in astonishment. "Neither do I condemn you. Go, and sin no more."[3]

Did you hear it? Did you hear what He said? "Neither do I condemn you!"

Do we understand that God does not wish to condemn us? That though His justice must demand the

---
1 John 8:7
2 Isaiah 6:3
3 John 8:11

ultimate penalty for our sins, it breaks His heart to do so? This is why He died! In that moment on a dusty bit of Israeli earth, the Messiah proclaimed His heart and the reason for His coming! He threw His mantle of protection, the ransom of His blood, over the woman and set her free.

This is not cheap grace, certainly! This is not something to be taken lightly! With His own life He bought grace for us. With His death He made mercy possible! It was on the promise of His full payment that David was forgiven his crimes, that Abraham and Moses talked with God, that Rahab was redeemed. Only because of His sacrifice does mercy reign in this world. Only because of His heart, the heart that broke and bled and stopped beating for our sake!

Understand! Every one of us who has come to God has come this way: thrown down to the ground, bloody and exposed and reeking with guilt. Every one of us has come with the voices of the Accuser and his demons cursing and taunting and shouting over our hanging heads, "The Law demands death. What do You say?"

Every one of us.

And to every one of us He has said it: "I do not condemn you. Go, and by my grace, sin no more." His is the right to condemn, His is the power. And because of His sacrifice, He has refused to exercise His right. He has refused to condemn us!

I hear joy in His voice, joy of such depth that I doubt any of us have ever fully experienced it. This is joy to make the stars sing, to send the Spirit of the Son of Man leaping and skipping and dancing upon the mountains. "Neither do I condemn you!"

Only one thing is asked of us: accept this grace. Accept it, and go forth from this place of confrontation with your sin—go forth a free man, or a free woman, and sin no more. Enter into this love and joy of your God, and learn to live by His Spirit.

And when you fall again, grace is still there.

Don't ever forget what He said.

"Neither do I condemn you. Go, and sin no more!"

* * *

"What then shall we say to these things? If God be for us, who can be against us?

"He that spared not his own Son, but delivered him up for us all, how shall he not with him also freely give us all things?

"Who shall lay anything to the charge of God's elect? It is God that justifieth.

"Who is he that condemneth? It is Christ that died, yea rather, that is risen again, who is even at the right hand of God, who also maketh intercession for us.

"Who shall separate us from the love of Christ? shall tribulation, or distress, or persecution, or famine, or nakedness, or peril, or sword?

"Nay, in all these things we are more than conquerors through him that loved us.

"For I am persuaded, that neither death, nor life, nor angels, nor principalities, nor powers, nor things present, nor things to come,

"Nor height, nor depth, nor any other creature, shall be able to separate us from the love of God, which is in Christ Jesus our Lord."

(Romans 8:31-39)

Circumstances...

"Circumstances are morally neutral. Circumstances should not be the chief focus of our prayers. The chief focus should be: how are we going to react to the circumstance—by turning toward God or by turning toward Satan, by letting God use the circumstance for our good or by letting Satan use it for our harm?"

Thomas Hale, from *On Being a Missionary*

notes from the author
APRIL 2003

Spring has arrived at last. The natural world is busily telling its resurrection story, as the death of winter is swallowed up in the budding of spring. At the same time, the season of Lent is drawing to a close. Easter is coming, the Day of Resurrection—the great Spring Day of the Lord.

This year, the pageant of death and resurrection has taken on a new dimension. A Middle Eastern country lies in ruin; waiting to be rebuilt. My prayers will be with Iraq on this Easter Sunday, for the light of new life is greatly needed there.

For me, Easter holds a thousand little significances. It gives me hope. The struggles of days past will be overcome, for He is risen. The darkness of winter will turn to the light of spring, for He is risen. Whatever you are struggling with, whatever challenges you face, let this season remind you that there is no reason to give up. He is risen.

Happy Easter!

Much love in the Messiah,

Rachel

Tyrants and Conquerors

A few short days ago, American soldiers rolled into Baghdad. Headlines proclaimed that freedom had come to Iraq. Radio and TV carried sounds and images of people singing and dancing in the streets. A Shiite leader declared that the tyrant had fallen; stone images of that tyrant toppled in the streets. Posters of Saddam Hussein were torn down by jubilant Iraqis who walked across the image of their former leader's face. A man ran alongside an army vehicle, shouting that Saddam had killed his family and crying, "Thank you, thank you, thank you."

Images like that warm our hearts. They make us glad that freedom has come to an oppressed people. They allow us to hope that the war will be over soon; that our boys will come home; and our world will become peaceful and predictable once more.

But the real story does not show a world at peace. Even now, looters continue to ransack Baghdad—and Mosul, and other cities—leaving destruction behind them. Government buildings are in flames. Thieves, both organized criminals and common people, take everything that is not nailed down. Even hospitals have been stripped of the equipment they need to function.

Many people live in fear of ethnic strife and revenge killings in a country where there is no police force to keep order. The picture of life in Iraq is not a pretty one. It reminds us that though the Iraqi people have gained one sort of freedom, in another sense they are still captives.

A tyrant has been toppled, yes. But a greater tyrant reigns still over the people of Iraq; a tyrant that has ruled every people and every culture for thousands of years. It is the tyrant called Sin.

Human beings put Saddam Hussein into power in Iraq many years ago, just as human beings welcomed sin into paradise thousands of years ago. Adam and Eve threw open the Gates of Eden to sin, and it was sin that caused the same Gates to slam shut behind them. They knew the truth of Paul's words: "Know ye not, that to whom ye yield yourselves servants to obey, his servants ye are to whom ye obey; whether of sin unto death, or of obedience unto righteousness?"[1]

For centuries, men and women have tried to create a perfect world—through politics, or art, or spirituality. But their efforts have proved in vain. Their hardest strivings are ultimately futile.

"What think ye of the Christ?" Jesus once asked the Pharisees. "Whose son is he?"

When they answered that the coming Messiah was to be David's son, Jesus quoted from the Psalms:

"The LORD said unto my Lord, sit thou on my right hand, till I make thine enemies a footstool. If David then call him Lord, how is he his son?"[2]

You see, no Son of David, be he the greatest artist, prophet, or king who ever lived, can ever save the

---

1   Romans 6:16
2   Matthew 22:42-45

world from sin. Only the Son of God can do that. For centuries people have looked to other human beings for salvation, but their hopes have been dashed because the leaders they looked to were themselves slaves of sin. No man made peace will ever last, because there is a destructive, murderous seed in every one of us. As long as the earth endures, it will breed tyrants, and traitors, and holocausts. It is inevitable, because the heart of every human being is "deceitful above all things, and desperately wicked: who can know it?"[1]

True freedom for the sons of men will not come through any son of David. Our Liberator must come from beyond this world; from outside of a race that has carried a deadly taint since Eden. If mankind is to be free, God Himself must intervene—and though much of the world is still unaware of it, He already has.

The prophet Isaiah wrote these words long before the coming of the Christ: "The people that walked in darkness have seen a great light: they that dwell in the land of the shadow of death, upon them hath the light shined."[2]

Two thousand years ago, He who is both Son of David and Son of God was born into a peasant family in a remote Roman province in the Middle East. While the world spun on unawares, busy with its political agendas and tribal wars, one man lived a perfect life. Those who followed Him knew only that He was like no other man they had ever known; but as time passed, their eyes were opened to His true nature. They saw Him work miracles; they saw Him speak with ancient prophets on a mountaintop; they heard Him speak the "words of life." They watched as He fulfilled the prophecies of the coming Messiah, and Peter confessed,

---

1 Jeremiah 17:9
2 Isaiah 9:2

"Thou art the Christ, the Son of the living God."[1]

While He was still a young man, the Son of God was falsely charged with blasphemy and cruelly executed. What those who killed Him did not realize was that they were really carrying out a part of God's plan of conquest. There on the cross, Jesus took on the tyrant—and defeated it. As Paul described it, "For what the law could not do, in that it was weak through the flesh, God sending his own Son in the likeness of sinful flesh, and for sin, condemned sin in the flesh"[2]

When Jesus rose from the dead three days later, the conquest was complete. Sin and Satan had been defeated. Those who throw themselves on the mercy of the Christ are delivered from the grip of the tyrant. The Holy Spirit has been given, so that those who are no longer slaves to sin might become the servants of God. Through the work of the Spirit, we are changed day by day into the likeness of the Liberator.

We are free, but all around us, the people of the earth are still in bondage. This year, as Easter reminds us of the death and resurrection of Christ, so the turmoil of war reminds us why it was necessary that He come. The tyrant still reigns over many hearts, but we have the message of liberation woven into our very souls. As the world continues to fight its battles, let us not forget the greater battle that is being fought all around us, in which we play a key part.

The world has been invaded. The tyrant has been conquered. It is up to us to take the message of liberation to the world.

---

1 Matthew 16:16
2 Romans 8:3

Hope

Hope, child, to-morrow, and to-morrow still,
    And every morrow hope; trust while you live.
Hope! Each time the dawn doth heaven fill,
    Be there to ask as God is there to give.

                Victor Hugo

For This Is the Will of God

"One act of thanksgiving made when things go wrong is worth a thousand when things go well."
- St. John of the Cross

At one time or another, we all find ourselves in circumstances beyond our control. Jobs are lost and once-stable finances reach a crisis point. Illness strikes. Churches lose sight of their vision and split into factions—and someone is always caught in the middle. Death comes.

And there is nothing we can do about it.

In crisis times, life becomes a complicated dance. We try to keep our feet in the path God has laid out for us, but His will isn't always clear. We are stepping in the dark. God is a God of light, and He does not keep us in the dark forever, but the fact remains that we often "see through a glass darkly."[1] Things will become clear—later. For now, we are called to put our hand squarely in the Lord's and step into the murk, believing that He will lead in the right direction. My problem is that I don't want to go where I can't see. I have a strong aversion to walking in faith. I want to know exactly what God is thinking and doing every second, so that not one of my own movements will be risky. I am

---
1 I Corinthians 13:12

a believer in the common misconception that if I know God's will, everything will go smoothly.

If you're doing a murky dance of your own, I have one piece of good news for you. I don't know if God wants you to go east or west, spend money here or save it there, pray for recovery or for strength to be weak. Those things you must discover for yourself. Those are the minutiae of God's will—the specific steps that will lead you in the right direction.

But there is a broader will of God, one that applies to you and to me no matter where we are. It's written in the Bible, in black and white, where anyone can see it. Obedience to it in the dark times, I find, brings an amazing amount of light. In this article, I'm only going to deal with one aspect of this greater will of God, and I hope that it encourages you as it does me.

It is God's will that we give thanks.

I'm not telling you that you must go leaping and skipping, strewing flowers in your wake, when you feel more like laying down to die. God does not ask us to manufacture emotions where there are none. God's will is not necessarily that you feel thankful—it is that you give thanks. The giving of thanks is an act of obedience, a matter of the will. Anyone can do it. And because God is a merciful, loving God, who knows what it's like to feel despondent and helpless (if you doubt it, read the Gospel accounts of Gethsemane), our act of thanksgiving is often followed by joy and peace, which are gifts of the Father and do not come out of our own strength.

"In everything give thanks," Paul says, "for this is the will of God concerning you."[1]

---

1   I Thessalonians 5:18

Something almost mystical happens when we give thanks in times of trouble. We proclaim to the world, to the devil, and to ourselves that God is still in control, that we are still His children, and that He is still blessing us—no matter what it may look like. The beauty of this is that it's true. He is in control. We are His children, and He is actively working everything for our good.[1]

When we choose to give thanks in a difficult situation, we choose to believe in God. We choose to believe in His promises. And because His promises are true, this choosing on our part brings light into darkness. Satan can do a great deal with a bitter heart. He can't do a thing with a heart that stubbornly insists on blessing God when the world seems to be falling apart.

Witness Job, whose own wife told him to "curse God and die."[2] True, the Book of Job does not seem at first glance to be a shining example of thankfulness. Job spends much of the book lamenting. But on closer examination, the oldest piece of writing in the Bible reveals a heart that is dead-set on being thankful. True, Job is at a loss to find anything to bless God about in the ash heap where he sits. So, he looks for something he can be thankful for—and finds it in the past.

"The Lord gave," he says—and how many beautiful memories are involved in that word "gave!" "The Lord gave, and the Lord hath taken away; blessed be the name of the Lord."[3]

A remembrance of God's faithfulness in days gone by not only gives us something to thank Him for, it also reminds us that the same faithfulness is working

---
1 Romans 8:28
2 Job 2:9
3 Job 1:21

now, and we will see the fruit of it in the future. As Job declares, "I know that my Redeemer lives, and he shall stand on the earth in the last day."

David also knew the secret of determined thankfulness. The shepherd king spent years on the run—from his king, from his conscience, from his son. Yet he continually exhorts himself and his followers to bless the Lord. Psalm after psalm begins with an admonition to thankfulness. Here are the opening verses to Psalms 103-106:

"Bless the Lord, O my soul: and all that is within me, bless his holy name."

"Bless the Lord, O my soul. O Lord my God, thou art very great; thou art clothed with honour and majesty."

"O give thanks unto the Lord; call upon his name: make known his deeds among the people."

"Praise ye the Lord. O give thanks unto the Lord; for he is good: for his mercy endureth forever."

Thanksgiving is one of the most powerful acts of faith we can possibly carry out. It is a grand announcement that our allegiance is fixed. It is a joyous defiance of Satan and all of his works. It is the singing of praises in prison that leads to the bursting of the prison doors.[1] It is the simple reaching of a child to a Father who is there, and that Father has never failed to reach right back.

Whatever circumstances you face today, or tomorrow; whatever decisions you now pray and mull over, do not forget the greater will of God.

Shout blessings in the desert caves that hide you from your enemies.

---

1 Acts 16:25

Sing praises in the prison cells where life has beaten and shackled you.

Remember His faithfulness on the ash heap; look to His promises when you are most in pain.

Give thanks, people of God.

And know that your Redeemer lives.

For the Ills That Might Have Been...

For the ills that might have been
But were neither heard nor seen,
For the fire that did not burn us,
Deeps that could not drown nor turn us,
For our daily blessings, Lord,
Be Thy name adored.

For the gentle joys that pass
Like the dew upon the grass,
New each morning, lighting duty
With a radiance and a beauty,
For our daily blessings, Lord,
Be Thy name adored.

For the storm that threatened loud
And then melted like a cloud,
Seeking to distress, confound us,
Met Thy great wings folded round us,
For our daily blessings, Lord,
Be Thy name adored.

Amy Carmichael, from *Gold Cord*

Beauty

Have you ever heard of speed dating? I read an article about it in a Christian magazine recently. Participants sign up for a speed dating event, held at a location near you. They gather in a meeting room and form their chairs in two circles—inner circle for the women, outer circle for the men. Each participant has a card with the other participants' names, with appropriate boxes to check for how highly you rate each person.

A supervisor with a stopwatch gets the night going. For a few seconds, each female participant speaks with a male participant. Just as the conversation gets going, the buzzer goes and the men move one place to the right—once again, ready, set, date.

There was a time when most girls believed in true love and eternal commitment—or if they didn't, at least we thought they should. The world was full of young romantics, sashaying around the kitchen humming "Someday My Prince Will Come." And while most of those young romantics were never exactly carried away by a knight in shining armour, at least they had an ideal to believe in.

Nowadays, that innocent belief in romance and true love has been replaced by yet another episode of The Bachelor. We date the way we shop for shoes, trying each new person on to see what criteria they meet—

are they comfortable? The right colour? Could I wear that with anything else in my closet? And most important—do they make me look good?

Some young people still believe in true love, albeit a skewered version of it. But the culture at large has taken romance, which for generations has been the most beautiful thing we knew, and sucked all the beauty out of it. Mystery is gone, replaced by immodesty. Faithfulness is gone, replaced by a credo that says we should only stay with someone as long as they make us happy.

The bottom line: romance, as presented by our culture, used to be beautiful. It isn't anymore.

This is not the only area of life that has suffered from a stripping-down of beauty. There was a time when family life was beautiful. Call to mind a scene from Little House On the Prairie. The Ingalls family sits around the fire at Christmas-time, stockings hung with care, snow blowing past the windows outside. It's a cold night, but it doesn't matter; there's love in the room, and that is beautiful; and when you're surrounded by such beauty, who cares what the weather's like outside?

Now call to mind a scene from *Married With Children. The Simpsons. Eight Simple Rules. Seventh Heaven,* even.

'Nuff said.

Whatever happened to beauty in our daily lives?

And then there are the artists: the singers, dancers, poets, painters, writers, and composers who once made it their business to make the whole world open their eyes to the beauty around them. There are still artists who present beauty in their work. But there are many more who seem concerned only with ugliness, with presenting jarring, bitter truths or twisted imaginations.

I am a writer; I spend five to six hours every day writing and reading. As a child I was drawn to reading because it opened up whole new worlds, and in those worlds there was beauty and wonder. Narnia and Middle-earth took my breath away. I rode on the back of George MacDonald's North Wind. I loved the silky darkness of an Indian night in Rudyard Kipling's Jungle Books. I loved to watch as time after time, the good guys defeated the bad ones.

But now? It grows harder and harder to find that kind of beauty in books. So many people use their creativity to create horrid things, disgusting things, jarring things; and more times than not, it's hard to tell the good guys from the bad.

All of this is simply to say that the world has changed, and not for the better. There is a dearth of beauty in the world, and it is a tragic loss.

It's easy enough to see the cause of it. God is the original of Beauty, and our culture has moved away from Him. The farther they go, the more warped their creations become. Instead of working as God works, to create that which is beautiful, wise, and good, they work as Satan does—twisting and perverting that which God has done.

As the world grows uglier, it is imperative that we as Christians pray the prayer of Moses:

"And let the beauty of the Lord our God be upon us: and stablish thou the work of our hands upon us; yea, the work of our hands establish thou it."[1]

---

[1] Psalm 90:17

In our lives, let the beauty of the Lord our God be upon us. In our families, in our friendships, in our romances and our marriages. In our art, let the beauty of the Lord our God be upon us. In our work. In our very souls.

The call of our time is to stand up in sharp contrast to the darkening world around, to shine a light into gross darkness:

"Arise, shine; for thy light is come, and the glory of the Lord is risen upon thee. For, behold, the darkness shall cover the earth, and gross darkness the people: but the Lord shall arise upon thee, and his glory shall be seen upon thee."[1]

I have seen beauty in dark places. I've seen it in the face of a wife and mother who gives and gives and gives for her children, who walks by her husband even when the road is mired in difficulty. I've seen it in young women who have kept themselves apart from the dating game, who have waited—and what a hard thing waiting can be!—until their prince came at last. I've seen it in the young men who have struggled to become worthy of a princess. I've seen it in my friends when they've clung to God through times of hurt and confusion. I've seen it at night, lying in bed, as I think back on my life and the people in it, and I think on the God who brought me this far. I've seen it in arms stretched out on a cross, in a scarred face, in the bloody footsteps of the Master.

Become a student of the Beautiful. Do beauty, think it, sing it, pray it. Stand against the tide of ugliness.

"Finally, brethren, whatsoever things are true, whatsoever things are honest, whatsoever things are

---

1 Isaiah 60:1-2

just, whatsoever things are pure, whatsoever things are lovely, whatsoever things are of good report; if there be any virtue, and if there be any praise, think on these things."[1]

---

1   Philippians 4:8

Beautiful

He stood, the youth they called the Beautiful,
At morning, on his untried battle-field,
And laughed with joy to see his stainless shield,
When, with a tender smile, but doubting sigh,
His lord rode by.

When evening fell, they brought him,
    wounded sore,
His battered shield with sword-thrusts gashed
    and rent,
And laid him where the king stood by his tent.
"Now art thou Beautiful," the master said,
And bared his head.

                  Annie M.L. Hawes

notes from the author

Recently I attended an event where a number of Christian performers got up to sing, one after the other. And I found it tiresome. Their abilities sparkled to varying degrees, but everything was noise. And then a man got up and sang a song to God, which proclaims, "You are more than enough for me." Suddenly the atmosphere changed. There was a stillness in the noise. There was worship.

So often we labour to create that which is only noise, and it becomes wearisome. When it does, look up and remember Him. Sing to Him. Pray to Him. Lay your head on His shoulder and rest. Let the Christmas Child turn your noise to worship.

Tinsel and Trappings and the Meaning of Life

It's December. Sweet month of mistletoe, holly, and ivy: there are carols in the air, bells on the street corners, reindeer on the roof. Madison Avenue has kicked into high gear. Hollywood is busy making movies which blow the message on silver trumpets: "Christmas is about family, Santa Claus, and Dr. Seuss." Every pastor in the nation is preaching a sermon from the first three chapters of the Book of Luke. Ten thousand families hang ten thousand decorations in ten thousand homes with ten thousand traditions.

All of which begs the question: what, exactly, is Christmas all about?

What comes to mind when *you* think of Christmas? Childhood memories. Sugar cookies. Sleigh rides and snowflakes and stockings by the fire. Presents. Family. Traditions. "Silent Night." All wonderful things, all important things (some more important than others)—but not one of the above answers the question. What is Christmas all about?

Last night in church we sang "Angels We Have Heard On High" and I thought about the shepherds on that very first Christmas, so very many years ago: I thought how they saw and heard such a wonder, and yet, they didn't fall into the trap we have fallen into. They did not go home and decorate angel trees; they didn't make angel cookies and sing angel carols. They knew that Christmas wasn't about angels. The angels knew it, too—they came for one reason, to point the hearts of men to a child in a manger.

Christmas is about Christ. It is about that Eternal Child who still brings light into the darkest of nights ("...beyond Jordan, in Galilee of the nations... The people that walked in darkness have seen a great light: they that dwell in the land of the shadow of death, upon them hath the light shined"[1]).

I love the tinsel and trappings of Christmas. Really I do. But the minute they cause me to lose sight of the Lord I love, they have done me a great disservice.

Up to this point, I am sure you all agree with me. But I don't want to stop yet; this truth, that Christmas is not about trappings but about Christ, goes beyond the holidays into the whole way we live our lives. You see, just as Christmas so often swallows Christ, so religion has often swallowed Him. Too many times our religion has become a song in which the music drowns out the words—a life that is all body and no heart.

What is your faith all about? Try and talk to people about the Lord and you will find yourself talking about prophecies and healings, programs and events, preachers and singers and services and denominations and mission agencies and the Christian next door who just doesn't understand Christianity. The fact is that God did not love the world so much that He sent First Baptist Church of Whereversville. He "so loved the world

---

1   Isaiah 9:1-2

that he gave his only begotten Son, that whosoever believeth in him should not perish, but have everlasting life."[1] Nor is the message, "Come unto the big Christian concert featuring sixteen Grammy award-winning singers and ye shall find rest." Jesus said, "Come unto *me*, all ye that labour and are heavy laden, and *I* will give you rest."[2]

Religion, with its traditions and observances, is not wrong in and of itself. We need it to help us frame the truth, to help us understand that which is too high for us. We kneel because it reminds us to pray; we sing because the song makes us think of freedom and beauty, and the Lord of both; we light candles to remind us of the Spirit's light inside of us. There is nothing wrong with any of this, until we stop using religion to lead us to Christ and start using it to lead us to itself.

When the children of Israel sinned against God in the desert and were poisoned by snakes, God instructed Moses to fashion a bronze snake and attach it to a pole, and those who looked at it would be healed. This strange statue was a symbol of the coming Messiah ("And as Moses lifted up the serpent in the wilderness, even so must the Son of man be lifted up: That whosoever believeth in him should not perish, but have eternal life"[3]). The Israelites kept the serpent for many years, until the time of King Hezekiah. In those days, the people had turned from God and had started worshiping the serpent itself—turning a reminder of God's grace into an idol. Hezekiah, in his zeal for the Lord, had the bronze snake destroyed.

Throughout history this pattern has repeated itself.

---

1 John 3:16
2 Matthew 11:28
3 John 3:14-15

People look to religion instead of looking to God. Those of us who come from a Protestant tradition think back to the Catholic Church of the Dark Ages and shake our heads, but our religious trappings have every bit as much potential to lead us astray—*if* we place our faith in them and not in Jesus. History proves this to be true. Those whose faith is in Christ live in love; those whose faith is in religion must live in judgment over others, for how else can they justify themselves?

My brothers and sisters, we must come back to the author and finisher of our faith, to our Messiah. We must fall at His feet and worship; we must walk in His footsteps. It is His voice we listen for. His character we pray for. His grace we live by. When you say the words "I am a Christian," what do they mean?

Take joy in the beauty of Christmas with all of its trappings, for they make children of us all. But do not allow the tinsel to outshine the child in a manger. When Christmas ends and a new year begins, do not scorn the established church and all it represents, but do not forget why we are here—do not forget *Who* we are here for. Christ must be all in all.

Join in the angelic host and proclaim it: "For unto you is born this day in the city of David a Saviour, which is Christ the Lord."

O Come, O Come, Emmanuel

O come, O come, Emmanuel
And ransom captive Israel,
That mourns in lonely exile here
Until the Son of God appear.

Rejoice! Rejoice! Emmanuel
Shall come to thee, O Israel.

O come, Thou Rod of Jesse, free
Thine own from Satan's tyranny;
From depths of hell Thy people save
And give them victory o'er the grave.

Rejoice! Rejoice! Emmanuel
Shall come to thee, O Israel.

O come, Thou Dayspring, come and cheer
Our spirits by Thine advent here;
And drive away the shades of night,
And pierce the clouds and bring us light!

Rejoice! Rejoice! Emmanuel
Shall come to thee, O Israel.

notes from the author
FEBRUARY 2003

Another year has rolled around, and once again the world is about to wake up to a day renowned for spasms of feeling, lonely delvings into ice cream buckets, extravagant, guilt-inspired gifts, and lacy pink hearts affixed to the tops of boxes of chocolate.

Yes, dear friends, it's Valentine's Day.

Let me say straight up that I like chocolates as much as the next girl, and anyone wishing to send me some is more than welcome. That said, however, I have a bone to pick with February 14. Despite its many declarations to the contrary, Valentine's Day is not about love.

I'm not entirely certain what it is about—increased profits for Hallmark and Dove, maybe—but it's not about love. The "love" it espouses is essentially about self. Its Hollywood attitude may hand you a basket of flowers today, but it'll leave you a heartbreak tomorrow. If you doubt me, listen to a group of teenage girls on Valentine's Day. They're in this to upstage their friends; to feed infatuation; to make sure their guy appreciates them. If they haven't got a guy (poor things), they're in for a night of tears and chocolate chip cookie dough ice cream.

This is not what love is about.

It's not that I think Valentine's Day is a bad idea.

Actually, I think it's wonderful to have a day in the year when we make a point of communicating our love and affection to the people who are important to us. Flowers and cards and dinners out and even chocolates are wonderful things. I myself have a Valentine date this year... my dear Uncle Stephen is taking me and a gaggle of sisters and cousins out.

So the problem isn't with the day itself. It's with the world's skewered idea of love.

As Christians, we ought to be holding the torch of true love high. Unfortunately, we're all too apt to get sucked into the world's counterfeit view of things. So, this Valentine's Day, I would like to use this space to remind myself and all of my faithful readers of the true meaning of the word "love."

I wish you all the best as you take this day to focus on true love and let the world know that there is indeed something higher.

Love in Christ,
Rachel

The Face of Love

There once lived a man whose name, earthly speaking, was Jesus.

Spiritually speaking, His name was Love.

Long ago, in the darkness of a distant age, Love looked far into the future. He went to His Father and said, "There is no other way. I will go to them. I will become one of them, and I will die for them."

In that time, before the foundations of the earth, Love was slain because of us.[1]

Many years later, when His now-human feet felt the pull of gravity and walked on hot Israeli sand, He said, "Greater love hath no man than this, that he lay down his life for his friends."

He knew what He was talking about. In spirit He had made the sacrifice long ago. In body He now came to carry it out on earth, and He did. He allowed Himself to be delivered into the cruel hands of men and sacrificed. Even now His sacrifice stands accepted in the heavenlies, and we have only to make it our own in order to receive forgiveness and righteousness.

To us He left His Spirit, that we might live out His law and His legacy of love.

"This is my commandment, that ye love one another."

---

1 I Peter 1:20

"By this shall all men know that ye are my disciples, if you have love one for another."

"Love your neighbour as yourself."

"Love your enemies, and do good to them that persecute you."

"Thou shalt love the Lord thy God with all thy heart, with all thy soul, with all thy mind, and with all thy strength."[1]

There are things we must understand about love if we want to follow His footsteps. For one thing, it is not the heady infatuation the world thinks it is. Love is deliberate. It is a choice. True, sometimes the choice is easy to make. A pair of beautiful eyes can coax us into it. A child's laughter sometimes causes our heart to overflow with it. A mother's careworn hands inspire it.

At other times, only the Spirit of God can bring it forth. Take Jesus' command to love our enemies, for example. No one ever "fell" in love with his persecutor. Jesus wasn't infatuated with the men whose hypocrisy and self-protection sent Him to the cross. His thoughts toward them were less than flowery—"Nest of vipers. White-washed tombs. Den of thieves"—such words are not the stuff of poetry and love letters. Yet He chose to love them. He prayed for their forgiveness on the cross.

Richard Wurmbrand, who endured fourteen years in prison in Communist Romania, wrote of the choice Jesus made that day, to love His enemies actively and wholly:

"When Jesus was on the cross, darkness fell upon Him and on the countryside. Soon an earthquake was

---

1   John 13:35, Matthew 22:39, Matthew 5:44, Mark 12:30

to follow. Jesus knew what was about to befall mankind because of His crucifixion. He saw in the darkness and the earthquake signs of God's judgment similar to what happened to Sodom and Gomorrah, and through His prayer He aborted the wrath of God. In that convulsion He became a lightning rod for us. God's wrath struck Him, and we the guilty were saved—all because He prayed."

That prayer was a deliberate choice to love His enemies. It was an expression of the love that carried Him to the cross in the first place—the love that was His nature, His whole soul.

Not only is love deliberate, it is active. When Jesus told us to love our enemies, He also gave us instructions on how to do so:

"Love your enemies,

bless them that curse you,

do good to them that hate you,

and **pray** for them which despitefully use you, and persecute you."[1]

Love is not a passive feeling over which we have no control. Love is action and choice. At times everything in us will stand behind the choice. At other times, our whole being will cry out against it. Yet obedience demands that we love no matter how hard or how easy the task. Love is the whole business of our lives as Christians.

What does love look like, practically speaking? It looks like Jesus. It looks like His work. Isaiah 58:6-8 beautifully describes a life that is given over to the business of love:

"Is not this the fast that I have chosen? to loose the

---
1 Matthew 5:44

bands of wickedness, to undo the heavy burdens, and to let the oppressed go free, and that ye break every yoke? Is it not to deal thy bread to the hungry, and that thou bring the poor that are cast out into thy house? when thou seest the naked, that thou cover him; and that thou hide not thyself from thine own flesh?

"Then shall thy light break forth as the morning, and thine health shall spring forth speedily: and thy righteousness shall go before thee; the glory of the Lord shall be thy rereward."

I have seen this kind of love in action before. I believe in God as I do because I know that His love is working in the world. I have been the hungry one who was fed by His people because they loved; the one who was clothed because they loved; the one who was given a roof over my head because they loved.

What does love look like?

It looks like a hug given to a difficult person because they are lonely and they need it.

It looks like the faithfulness of a mother who gives her life to husband and children.

It looks like laughter when things are going wrong.

It looks like unceasing prayer; for family, and for friends, and for missionaries, and for the lost, and for the hated, and for the outcasts, and for the prisoners, and for the enemy.

It looks like a drink of water to a thirsty man.

It looks like a loaf of bread to a starving child.

It looks like sacrifice.

It looks like hard work.

It looks like patience.

It looks like kindness.

It looks like humility.

It looks like Jesus.

We fear love, as we fear all things that are truly holy and heavenly. We fear it because it makes us vulnerable. It leaves us open to hurt. Of course it does. Isn't the Christian life about trusting God with our whole lives? Isn't it about tearing down our hardened walls and letting Him be our protector and judge? When we cease trying to protect ourselves and begin instead to give of ourselves, then we are beginning to walk the path of love.

Love recognizes that it needs others. In God's Kingdom there is no such thing as a lone wolf. God's great desire for us is that we might become one—and it is through our union, through our love, that the world will know that we are His. It is through our love that they will believe that our Lord lives and is in us.

Says George MacDonald, "We wrong those near us in being independent of them. God himself would not be happy without his Son. We ought to lean on each other, giving and receiving—not as weaklings but as lovers."

The world needs lovers now as never before. Jesus Himself prophesied that in the iniquitous last days, the love of many would wax cold.[1] It is for us to keep love strong. It is for us to minister to the hungry, the cold, the outcast, and the lonely. It is for us to minister to our Lord by keeping the cords of love strong in His body.

The Wailing Aztecs, a Canadian folk band, once recorded a song which stated, "We don't need another love song. All we need is love."

---

[1] Matthew 24:12

My brothers and sisters, it is up to us to write a love song with our lives. We cannot do it on our own power—the world is a place of hate and of selfishness, and it will always do its best to beat us down—but the Spirit of Love lives in us.

What does love look like?

To the world, it looks like you.

Collected Thoughts on Love

For strength we ask
For the ten thousand times repeated task,
The endless smallnesses of every day.

No, not to lay
My life down in the cause I cherish most,
That were too easy. But, whate'er it cost,
To fail no more
In gentleness toward the ungentle, nor
In love toward the unlovely, and to give,

Each day I live
To every hour with outstretched hand its meed
Of not-to-be-regretted thought and deed.

Agnes Ethelwyn Wetherald

"More and more I feel that love is the golden secret of life. The very air of heaven is love, for God is love and love never fails. So go on loving not only the loveless but the unlovable, the difficult, the perplexing, the disappointing—unto the end."

Amy Carmichael, from *Candles in the Dark*

"Set me as a seal upon thine heart, as a seal upon thine arm: for love is strong as death; jealousy is cruel as the grave: the coals thereof are coals of fire, which hath a most vehement flame. Many waters cannot quench love, neither can the floods drown it: if a man would give all the substance of his house for love, it would utterly be contemned."

> Song of Solomon 8:6-7

"If I cannot in honest happiness take the second place (or the twentieth); if I cannot take the first without making a fuss about my unworthiness, then I know nothing of Calvary love.

"If I take offence easily, if I am content to continue in a cool unfriendliness, though friendship be possible, then I know nothing of Calvary love.

"If monotony tries me, and I cannot stand drudgery; if stupid people fret me and little ruffles set me on edge; if I make much of the trifles of life, then I know nothing of Calvary love.

"If souls can suffer alongside, and I hardly know it, because the spirit of discernment is not in me, then I know nothing of Calvary love.

"If I slip into the place that can be filled by Christ alone, making myself the first necessity to a soul instead of leading it to fasten upon Him, then I know nothing of Calvary love.

"If I wonder why something trying is allowed, and press for prayer that it may be removed; if I cannot be trusted with any disappointment, and cannot go on in peace under any mystery, then I know nothing of Calvary love."

Amy Carmichael, from *If*

"If I speak with the tongues of men and of angels, but do not have love, I have become a noisy gong or a clanging cymbal. If I have the gift of prophecy, and know all mysteries and all knowledge; and if I have all faith, so as to remove mountains, but do not have love, I am nothing. And if I give all my possessions to feed the poor, and if I surrender my body to be burned, but do not have love, it profits me nothing.

"Love is patient, love is kind and is not jealous; love does not brag and is not arrogant, does not act unbecomingly; it does not seek its own, is not provoked, does not take into account a wrong suffered, does not rejoice in unrighteousness, but rejoices with the truth;

"Bears all things, believes all things, hopes all things, endures all things. Love never fails."

I Corinthians 13:1-8a (NASV)

Voices

"The earth is the Lord's, and the fulness thereof; the world, and they that dwell therein."

Psalm 24:1

There are fireflies in the trees tonight. They light up the dusk in a thousand little candle-flickers. There are fireflies in the trees; and the cicadas and the crickets and the frogs are chirping, and an inordinately large beetle, which drones as it flies like a tiny dive-bomber, keeps flying up and hitting its head on my window screen. It hits the screen and bounces off, flies around in circles until it gets its bearings back, and then does the whole thing over again.

Yes, and tonight I took a walk down the dirt road that looks almost white in the dusk, and I watched the deer bound across the field in a flash of white tail and leaping grace, while the beetles droned over my head and the first stars came out, and the smell of fresh-cut grass and wildflowers filled the air.

Here, where I live, I bless God every time I step out the door. Summer has come with its thousand secrets and I am here to see it and hear it and smell it and think how it all reminds me of Him.

The world, whose friendship is enmity with God, may have little to do with the Creator. But the earth is still His. He is everywhere in it. He rides on the wings of the wind; He brings the rain and calls forth the harvest; He feeds the ravens and the lions; He is there when the deer calve.

Two years ago I lived in a very different wilderness: the Mojave Desert of California. There, too, we lived on a dirt road; and there, too, I would take walks in the dusk while coyotes called and ravens settled in on Joshua trees for the night. Life wasn't always easy out there, no more than it is here, and sometimes when I walked I would do so with my head bowed, my eyes cast down, the dirt all I could see.

And then one day I looked up, and there were the mountains: snowcapped, glowing white and pink and purple in the sunset. The lights of the town sparkled in the dark foothills, but the light of the sun was still on the peaks. I heard the word then, and I give it to you now: look up! Look up and know that no matter how great your trials, God is bigger; He is stronger; He will outlast them all, and so, child of the Mountain-God, will you.

There was another walk down that road when the sky was brown with dust. Even the mountains were hazy. But as I walked I saw clouds rolling in, and thunder sounded off in the distance; it began to rain, and as it did the dirt was washed down out of the sky, leaving streaks of clear blue behind it. Then again there was a word, and I wrote a song about it:

Dust billows from the world around

And gathers itself in my soul
I will lay this burden down
As You come, and make me whole

O Desert Soul, you've gathered
So much pain
Now hear the thunder sound as you
Call on His name!

And let the water fall down and down...

When I was very young I would sit in the crook of a wild cherry tree and listen to the birches around as they talked to each other. Of course I knew their conversations were all in my head; I was making them up. But the earth and all its creatures do talk—if you listen you can hear them.

And what do they speak of?

As Spring follows Winter without fail, the voices of melting snow and sprouting leaf speak of resurrection.

As the birds believe that the earth will supply them with food; as the fields believe that rain will come; the songs of the birds and the scent of the wildflowers teach us trust.

As the butterfly that lives for a brilliant day and the tree that stands in silence for a thousand years, the quiet acceptance of life teaches us contentment with the time and the calling God has given.

The whole earth is a monument to the One who made it. So go outside. Take a deep breath—through your nose, so you can smell the summer air. Look around you. And listen. Always listen. The earth is talking.

What does it have to say to you?

Consider the Ravens

Lord, according to thy words,
I have considered thy birds;
And I find their life good,
And better, the better understood;
Sowing neither corn nor wheat
They have all that they can eat;
Reaping no more than they sow
They have more than they could stow;
Having neither barn nor store,
Hungry again they eat more.

But this is when there blow no storms,
When berries are plenty in winter, and worms,
When feathers are rife, with oil enough
To keep the cold out and send the rain off;
If there come, indeed, a long, hard frost
Then it looks as though thy birds were lost.

But I consider further and find
A hungry bird has a free mind;
He is hungry to-day, but not to-morrow,
Steals no comfort, no grief doth borrow;
This moment is his, thy will hath said it,

The next is nothing till Thou hast made it.

The bird has pain, but has no fear—
Which is the worst of any gear;
When cold and hunger and harm betide him,
He does not take them and stuff inside him;
Content with the day's ill he has got,
He waits just, nor haggles with his lot;
Neither jumbles God's will
With driblets from his own still.

But I see, in my endeavour,
The birds here do not live forever;
That cold or hunger, sickness or age,
Finishes their earthly stage;
The rooks drop in cold nights,
Leaving all their wrongs and rights;
Birds lie here and birds lie there
With their feathers all astare;
And in thine own sermon, thou
That the sparrow falls dost allow.

It shall not cause me any alarm,
For neither so comes the bird to harm
Seeing our Father, thou hast said,
Is by the sparrow's dying bed;
Therefore it is a blessed place,
And a sharer in high grace.

It cometh therefore to this, Lord:

I have considered thy word;
And henceforth will be thy bird.

> George MacDonald

Commonplace

"A commonplace life," we say, and we sigh;
    But why should we sigh as we say?
The commonplace sun in the commonplace sky
    Makes up the commonplace day.
The moon and the stars are commonplace things,
And the flower that blooms and
    the bird that sings,
But dark were the world and sad our lot
If the flowers failed and the sun shone not;
And God, who studies each separate soul
Out of commonplace lives makes
    his beautiful whole.

                Anonymous

Light of the World, Salt of the Earth

*"Ye are the salt of the earth:
but if the salt have lost his savour,
wherewith shall it be salted?
it is thenceforth good for nothing,
but to be cast out,
and to be trodden underfoot of men.*

*"Ye are the light of the world.
A city that is set on a hill
cannot be hid.
Neither do men light a candle,
and put it under a bushel,
but on a candlestick;
and it giveth light to all that are in the house.*

*"Let your light
so shine before men,
that they may see your good works,
and glorify your Father
which is in heaven."*

Matthew 5:13-16

> *"Who knoweth whether thou art come*
> *to the kingdom*
> *for such a time as this?"*
>
> Esther 4:14b

> *"Remember Lot's wife."*
>
> Luke 17:32

We live in troubled times. Do you doubt it? Watch the news. The kings of the earth take council together to decide if our sons and daughters will go to another weary war; while at home, God is mocked, the innocent are murdered, families are ripped to shreds, and children gun each other down and laugh.

Galadriel's words at the opening of the movie Lord of the Rings seem all too appropriate for our own time: "The world is changed. I feel it in the water. I feel it in the earth. I smell it in the air. Much that once was is lost, for none now live who remember it. Rumour grows of a shadow in the east; whispers of a nameless fear."

This nation was once godly in its heart and ways, but now the last vestiges of that heritage fast disappear, crushed by the war which has been waged against it in the hallowed halls of society for decades. Truly, much that once was is lost. We live in what some call the "post-Christian era," a time in which men have become too wise for God and so are doomed to reap the rewards of their own foolishness.

In Tolkien's story, though, hope was not lost—it lived on in small bands of the faithful: of those in whose breasts still beat the heart of heroism; in those who clung to beauty and goodness and refused to forget that better days had been; and in the hobbits, a people so small and insignificant, so childlike, that only the forces of good could make any use of them. These few faced evil with nothing except hope and determination on their side, and they won.

Neither is hope lost in our world. Here, too, the heroes are those who cling to goodness—who cling to God—who trust simply and do their duty with all the courage that comes from throwing oneself on the Lord of Heaven.

Such heroes live and work in every corner of the globe. They are the missionaries who dare disease and devil alike to stop them; who trek into the darkest corners of life and carry with them the candle flame of the living gospel. They are the families who cling to each other; who honour one another while all the world tells them to cut ties and seek independence; who love one another while all the world tells them to bury love in selfishness; who commit to one another when even their own souls wish to give up.

They are the young people who stand up for purity in a perverted nation. They are the persecuted Christians who suffer and hunger and die, and count it all worth it for the sake of the cross. They are those who remember a man named Jesus in all they say and in all they do; who make their lives a memorial to One who raised the dead and yet gave His own soul to death for our sakes, One who Was and Is and Is to Come.

They are the light of the world, and they are the salt of the earth.

If you are a Christian, you are one of them.

It is easy to forget our calling, as we endlessly follow the daily circle of sleep-eat-work-sleep. It is easy to look at the little we have and fail to look beyond it to the greater purposes of God (though God does not fail to see past appearances, and "out of commonplace lives make His beautiful whole").

We share the calling of every God-follower who has ever lived, from the time of Adam till now. As light we illumine darkness; as salt we battle the corroding influences of the world. Sometimes this is a conscious battle, more often it is not. But it is being fought nevertheless, and the consequences of it affect everything around us.

It is my belief that no society can ever be spoiled completely while a witness remains in it for God, because salt keeps the meat from rotting. For this reason Sodom and Gomorrah could not be destroyed while the righteous remained within their gates; and Lot's wife, who had "lost her savour," became a pillar of salt when she longed to return, in one of the most ironic scenes in the Bible. For this reason the people of God will be taken out of the world before the final judgment comes upon it.

But for now, we are here; and we have work to do. Have you ever looked around you and wondered when God was going to do something about the corruption you see? The fact is, He has done something about it—He has placed you in the midst of it.

There is no formula for how to be effective as salt

and light in the world. Each one of us has a separate calling, uniquely formed by God for unique purposes. If we are to be effective in changing the world around us, only one thing is required: faithfulness. It is required that we do the work that is given us to do with our whole heart and that we cease not to seek Him and walk in His ways. If we do, our own closeness to the Father will spill over; as an old Hasidic proverb states, "There are people who can utter words of prayer with true fervour, so that the words shine like a precious stone whose radiance shines of itself. Then again there are people whose words are nothing but a window that has no light of its own, but only lets the light in and shines for that reason."

As Christians, we are to let the light in with everything that we do.

We live in troubled times, and so it is good that we remember who we are in God's will. No candle is needed when the sun shines high; but in the darkness, the smallest flame can illuminate a world. This world is dark and getting darker, and so it is for us to go to God and surrender ourselves anew; asking that He use us in the small things of life, so that the great things may be transformed.

A prayer is a small thing; a very small thing, but prayer shakes nations and always has. When next you see a grievous thing, don't shake your head and walk away—bow your head, and add your voice to the cry of the watchmen:

> *"I have set watchmen upon thy walls,*
> *O Jerusalem,*
> *which shall never hold their peace day nor night:*

> *ye that make mention of the* Lord,
> *keep not silence,*
> *And give him no rest,*
> *till he establish,*
> *and till he make Jerusalem a praise in the earth."*

Isaiah 62:6-7

And love is a small thing, kindled in small hearts; but it grows until nothing can stand in its way:

> *"For love is strong as death;*
> *Jealousy is cruel as the grave:*
> *the coals thereof are coals of fire,*
> *which hath a most vehement flame.*
>
> *"Many waters cannot quench love,*
> *neither can the floods drown it."*

Song of Solomon 8:6b-7a

Even so, an apology is a small thing. It is no great thing to humble oneself, to ask forgiveness; it is no great thing to work with those we do not agree with; it is no herculean task to overlook annoyances and let love "cover a multitude of sins." But these things create unity, which, together with love, shouts the gospel with such a great voice that it is a deaf man indeed who cannot hear it:

> *"That they all may be one;*

> *as thou, Father, art in me, and I in thee,*
> *that they also may be one in us;*
> *that the world may believe that thou hast sent me.*
>
> *"And the glory which thou gavest me I have given them;*
> *they they may be one,*
> *even as we are one;*
>
> *"I in them, and thou in me,*
> *that they may be made perfect in one;*
> *and that the world may know that thou hast sent me,*
> *and hast loved them,*
> *as thou hast loved me."*
>
> John 17:21-23

When Jesus came to Earth some two thousand years ago, God bypassed the rulers of the world's mightiest Empire and worked His will through a dumb priest and an elderly woman; through a camel-haired prophet; through a carpenter and a teenage girl. That girl sang the Magnificat, and rejoiced in the day of small things: "My soul doth magnify the Lord, And my spirit hath rejoiced in God my Saviour. He hath put down the mighty from their seats, and exalted them of low degree. He hath filled the hungry with good things; and the rich he hath sent empty away." (Luke 1:46-47, 52-53)

I am a small thing, and you are a small thing; a pinch of spice here and a candle flicker there; but if we are faithful and surrendered, God will work wonders through us. This is our calling. As the world gets darker, I pray that we will shine all the brighter. As you go about the "endless smallnesses of every day," remember whose hands you are in and resolve to be His in everything.

> *Worship, therefore, at the midnights*
> *When the stars hide.*
> *Worship in the storms till love*
> *Makes thunder whimper and grow quiet*
> *And listen to your whispered hymns.*
>
> Calvin Miller, from *A Requiem for Love*

Threefold Love

Even a God
When in human flesh,
Needs a touch.

He rose from the water,
Troubled with visions
Of a future dying day.

The Father saw His loneliness
He nodded to the Spirit,
And they reached down
And touched Him.

"Now when all the people were baptized, it came to pass, that Jesus also being baptized, and praying, the heaven was opened, And the Holy Ghost descended in bodily form like a dove upon him, and a voice came from heaven, which said, Thou art my beloved Son; in thee I am well pleased."

Luke 3:21-22

notes from the author

Today is Sunday, and when I got back from church I went downstairs and listened to a recorded message given my grandmother, who passed away last December. I loved it. She had a great deal of good to say—and it was just good to hear her voice again.

At the beginning of the message she urged her listeners to encourage each other. "Encourage people every chance you get." Don't wait until it's too late to say what you feel, say it now. Life beats us all up plenty, so we should really do our best to lift each other up.

A Dance With Mystery

"I think how a yearning
Kept on returning to move me
Down roads I'd never have chosen
Half the time frozen
Too numb to feel.

"I know it was stormy
Hope it was for me a learning
Blood on the road wasn't mine, though
Someone that I know
Has walked here before."

from *"Here by the Water"* by Jim Croegaert

Every day we live is one more step into the unknown. Stability, normality: they are myths, perpetuated by a world of individuals who would not have the courage to live without them. If New Yorkers could have foreseen what would happen after the sun rose on September 11, 2001, how many would have possessed the strength to get out of bed that morning? Every one of us dances with Mystery; it is an exhilarating, sometimes terrifying, dance—because we cannot know how it will end.

But we, who are the people of God, need not fear the unknown. The road ahead is covered in mist, that much is true, but the road is not really unknown. There is One who has walked it before us.

"He calleth his own sheep by name, and leadeth them out," Jesus said, "and when he putteth forth his own sheep, *he goeth before them*, and the sheep follow him, because they know his voice."[1]

Jesus here spoke of one He called "the Good Shepherd"—Himself. "He goeth before them." Jesus never asked anyone to go into uncharted waters alone. He asked only that they follow Him, trusting that the way ahead of them has been prepared by the Master.

The disciples knew this. I love the words which the angel spoke to the women at the empty tomb: "Go your way, tell his disciples and Peter that he goeth before you into Galilee: there shall ye see him, as he said unto you."[2] It is the same for us. He has gone before us; if we would see Him, we must follow.

And so we join hands with the cloaked spectre of Mystery and dance, unafraid, down the pathways of life. Those who do not believe cannot know what the future holds for them. And while we do not know the exact circumstances of ours, we do know this—for us, the name of Mystery is the Will of God, and that Will is good and perfect.

Do not suppose that this means the way ahead is all through green pastures and quiet valleys. The perfect will of God led Jesus to Gethsemane, to the cross.

---

1 John 10:4
2 Matthew 28:7

As Amy Carmichael asks, "Can he have followed far, who has no wound nor scar?" But it also led Him to the Resurrection, to Galilee, and to the endless skies. It is the same for us. If God leads us into the Valley of the Shadow of Death, certainly He will lead us out again.

There is another place the Spirit of God may lead. I have been there, and the greatest struggle while there is a struggle with doubt—for it is very hard to recognize any reason or plan of God underneath the deadness of the surroundings. I speak of the Desert, where every wind scorches and the sun causes illusions that parade doubts through our minds, where the path is seemingly lost in endless sand. But even here He has gone before us, as Luke tells the story: "And Jesus was led by the Spirit into the wilderness."[1]

It is not an easy thing to understand, this leading of the Spirit into the wilderness. For oftentimes the first person we meet there is the old Adversary himself, Satan, who thrives on deadness. It is hard to know why we must endure the tempting of the devil, in this place where there is so little to sustain us. But God has His reasons, never doubt it. Moses understood the reasons better than most, and he gave them to the children of Israel:

"And thou shalt remember all the way which the LORD thy God led thee these forty years in the wilderness, to humble thee, and to prove thee, to know what was in thine heart, whether thou wouldest keep my commandments, or no. And he humbled thee, and suffered thee to hunger, and fed thee with manna, which thou knewest not, neither did thy fathers know; that he might make thee know that man doth not live by bread only, but by every word that proceedeth out of

[1] Luke 4:1

the mouth of the LORD doth man live."[1]

Learn the lessons of the desert when you find yourself there, for there is more richness in that arid soil that you could ever imagine. And do not fear: God does not intend to leave you there. No, His plan is to bring you out: "...into a good land, a land of brooks of water, of fountains and depths that spring out of valleys and hills."[2] May you leave the wilderness as Jesus left it: "And Jesus returned in the power of the Spirit into Galilee: and there went out a fame of him through all the region round about."[3]

Do not be afraid to dance with Mystery. Trust that God has a plan for your life, and follow Him boldly. Keep your eyes open, for the nail-scarred footprints of the Master are everywhere, proclaiming to all with eyes to see that He has been here.

Mystery does not remain cloaked forever. Bit by bit the mist falls away and Mystery becomes Story, written in the saga of history forever. When your life is over, may you look back on the dance of life in awe of the Presence who went before you, who guarded behind you, and who walked beside you even when you were sure He was not there.

---

1 Deuteronomy 8:2-3
2 Deuteronomy 8:7
3 Luke 4:14

No Scar?

Hast thou no scar?
No hidden scar on foot, or side, or hand?
I hear thee sung as mighty in the land,
I hear them hail thy bright ascendant star,
Hast thou no scar?

Hast thou no wound?
Yet I was wounded by archers, spent,
Leaned Me against a tree to die; and rent
By ravening beasts that compassed Me, I swooned:
Hast thou no wound?

No wound? No scar?
Yet, as the Master shall the servant be,
And pierced are the feet that follow Me;
But thine are whole: can he have followed far
Who has no wound nor scar?

Amy Carmichael, from *Toward Jerusalem*

notes from the author

A few weeks ago I sat in the back row at a church service, and I almost could have cried for the isolation I felt. It was a strange sort of isolation—I felt the presence of the Lord with me, but in spite of the church building and not because of it. In the sermon, the speaker asked us to raise our hands if we were "hot toward God," "cold," or "lukewarm." He gave a description for each of the three, and while hands went up all around me, mine remained down. Not because I was trying to be difficult—I was crying out to the Lord to let me connect—but because none of the descriptions fit my life. The Christianity inside that building at that moment felt strangely divorced from my life outside the walls.

I love the Church. I love the Bride Christ died for. This article is not meant to be a tirade against her. Rather, it is a lament for her. I cry for the Church in America the same way I cry for a teenage girl who has buried her soul under makeup. Her spirit is beautiful. She has so much to offer—but she has become so concerned with the outward appearances of things that she has failed to ever get past them.

The boxes I talk about in this article aren't just a matter of physical walls, though that is the metaphor I use. Nor is it only "church organizations" that put them up. The walls are inside me, too. When I sit in the back at a service and struggle, I am not only crying out for release from the walls others have made, but from the box inside me.

I questioned whether or not to use this article in Letters. It is a major departure from my usual style; a sort of poetic heart's cry. And I didn't want anyone to feel judged or belittled. But I chose to use it because I know that the cry of my heart has an echo in you.

Seeking Him,
Rachel

Why Can't We Sing?

I sit in a church, and look to the ceiling. Churches have ceilings—four walls, and a floor. Even so, a church should not feel like a box.

"Your relationship with God fits into one of these three categories," says the preacher. "Raise your hand and tell me what door you live behind—1, 2, or 3." The people bow their heads and close their eyes and raise their hands, and the walls of the box close in tighter. I look up to the ceiling and my eyes try to penetrate the grey. I Am is not here! Not trapped in this room! He fills all the starry sky. Oh, to fly with Him! Up from the building, out from the boxes. My life is not behind a door. It does not fit into neat little wrapping any more than my God does!

"Stand and sing," the preacher says. "Stand and worship God." And I try to sing.

> *Manufactured music without melody.*
> *We drum and we drone and we raise our hands high.*
> *But we're trying to sing!*
> *Lord, why can't we sing?*
> *Our music falls short of a song.*

There is a Woman. Christ loves her. She "looketh forth as the morning, fair as the moon, clear as the sun, and terrible as an army with banners."[1] She is the Church, the Bride, and I also love her. But I see her not yet a woman—a girl only, one who peers into the mirror and frowns at the scars Jesus loves. She frowns and tries to cover herself up. She wants to look like a cover girl. She wants the world to think she is beautiful. And she covers the music in her soul with all the world's visible noise.

> *"Do your makeup, do your hair,*
> *"Bow your head, say your prayers."*
> *Set us free from the world!*
> *From the tyranny of paint!*
> *We're trying to sing!*
> *Lord, why can't we sing?*
> *Our music falls short of a song.*

"Are you a good Christian?" the preacher asks. "Read your Bible, say your prayers. Smile at your neighbour and say the magic words." We're on fire for God, lighting little matchsticks that flicker in wind and die under water. Yet in our God a fire rages—a mighty kiln, an all-Consuming Fire. Into the depths we are called, where the Fourth Man waits to meet us, "one like the Son of God."[2] Instead we comfort ourselves in church and sing with the youth group and pretend that this is what we are called to, and divorce ourselves further from reality.

---

1   Song of Solomon 6:10
2   Daniel 3:25

"We're on fire for God"
But our fire burns pale
Like neon lights on white city walls.
But where is the burning?
The deep-seated fire?
Our music falls short of a song.

There! Outside the church walls a woman is weeping! She has chosen the Right. She has chosen Rejection. The world has turned its back and she is hurting. Real pain. Real suffering. But there, can you see it? The flame flickering in her soul. Her teardrops are the colour of fire.

There! With the children, learning to love. A young man is breaking. He is letting go of the Noise and letting silence in. And there in the silence, deep in his soul—can you hear it? The song is beginning to stir. Soon he will sing. And the music will move the stars to weep and to rejoice.

There! On the green hill, under the moon. An old man is looking up, up to the sky, and thinking, and dreaming, and knowing at last that I AM THAT I AM is there. The top of the box is lifting slowly. Fire and song mingle deep within his soul. Soon the box will fade completely, and then he will fly.

There! In the dirt of the world! In the pain of life! In the deepest things of soul and sky! There I can see her, the Woman that Christ loves, the Bride that He died to make her.

So I bow my head in the box and the music drones on.

Manufactured music without melody.

Then I smile and lift my eyes.

We drum and we drone and we lift our hands high.

Under the noise I know she is there...

But we're trying to sing!
Lord, why can't we sing?

 The Woman I love is there, trying to sing. And someday she'll learn, and she'll cast off the noise.
 For the first time she'll fly: she'll sing, and she'll fly.
 In fields of fire she'll run, and she'll see Him. He'll hold out His hand, and she'll take it.
 They'll dance.

Manufactured music without melody
We drum and we drone and we raise our hands high.
But we're trying to sing!
Lord, why can't we sing?
Our music falls short of a song.

Bondage

"A man is in bondage to whatever he cannot part with that is less than himself."

George MacDonald

Love Touches

Jesus stepped into the water where His cousin John awaited Him. As He slipped under the surface, perhaps the water whispered to Him of the future. Perhaps He heard the words of Paul, yet to be spoken: "We are buried with him by baptism into death..."[1]

The touch of death shivered through the water that day.

When Jesus rose from the water His eyes swept the shores, where many familiar faces peered out at him. Perhaps He heard one part of His life close resolutely behind Him. As He looked at the faces of poor man and publican, scribe and sinner, He knew what was coming. The days were gone in which it would be said of Him, "And he grew in favour with God and man."[2] No longer would the favour of men be His. Soon these old familiar faces would twist with hatred and with outrage at His words; hands He had known since His youth would try to cast Him off a cliff.

The shades of "Crucify Him" passed over the faces of the crowd.

Jesus did not consider turning back. His Father's will was clear; and it was just as clear that He would

---
1 Romans 6:4
2 Luke 2:52

fulfill it. Such was the love of Son to Father, that the disapproval of His whole human family did not matter next to the wishes of His God.

Even so, it must have been lonely in the water that day.

God the Father knew that it was. He knew the shadows that burdened His son. He knew the sting that comes with losing the approval of people who ought to stand loyal. God the Holy Spirit understood, as well, and He also ached for the Son.

So together, the Father and the Spirit reached down to the lonely One.

The Holy Spirit touched Him. Not an indescribable, spiritual touch: a physical one. It was a touch with soft feathers and black eyes; the touch of a dove.

God the Father spoke to Him. "You are my beloved Son," He reminded Jesus. "And I am well pleased with You."[1]

No one understood that day but John the Baptist, and even he was never quite sure what to make of what he had seen. All he knew was that he had seen great holiness at work.

He had seen great love.

Many years ago, an English Christian tried to capture the love of God in words, and he managed about as well as most of us do:

> "Could we with ink the ocean fill,
> And were the skies of parchment made.
> Were every stalk on earth a quill,
> And every man a scribe by trade,

---

[1] Mark 1:11

"To write the love of God above
Would drain the ocean dry.
Nor could the scroll contain the whole,
Tho' stretched from sky to sky.

"O love of God, how rich and pure!
How measureless and strong!
It shall forevermore endure
The saints' and angels' song."

That song is beautiful and poetic and very, very true; and it meant a great deal to the one who wrote it. But it gives only one side of God's love: the mystery side. It does not transmit the truth of God's practical love—the kind of love that touches and speaks to one who needs it.

God's love reaches not only to the stars, but to us. It touches people in concrete ways. It doesn't only delve to the lowest hell, but it lives and moves in slums and tenements and refugee camps. It is this sort of love that we must get hold of if we want to be of any use to God in this world. A man who is dying of thirst does not care to hear that God's love is deeper than the ocean, but he will hear—he must hear—that God's love can be found in a glass of water. A child without family is not comforted to hear that God's love "is like a river," but he does want to know that God's love is like a hug.

God's love is mystery, yes, but it is also immensely practical. If we as Christians claim to love each other, as Jesus commanded us to, we must live that love not in the far-off heights of noble thoughts and speculations, but in the day-to-day challenges of bad tempers and dull ordinariness, of tears and laughter, of inner needs and outer hunger. And if we are to demonstrate the love of God to the world, it will not be in a pie-in-the-sky, metaphysical way, but in earthly practicality.

If you read the Gospels, you will see that the love of God touches. It heals. It feeds. It washes feet. Jesus did not just talk about the love of His Father; He demonstrated it.

Go and do likewise.

Confession of the Sisters of the Common Life

My Vow.
Whatsoever Thou sayest unto me, by Thy grace I will do it.
My Constraint.
Thy love, O Christ, my Lord.
My Confidence.
Thou art able to keep that which I have committed unto Thee.
My Joy.
To do Thy will, O God.
My Discipline.
That which I would not choose, but which Thy love appoints.
My Prayer.
Conform my will to Thine.
My Motto.
Love to live: Live to love.
My Portion.
The Lord is the portion of mine inheritance.

Teach us, good Lord, to serve Thee more faithfully; to give and not to count the cost; to fight and not to heed the wounds; to toil and not to seek for rest; to labour and not to ask for any reward, save that of knowing that we do Thy will, O Lord our God.

> Amy Carmichael, from *Gold Cord*

Home

*T*he small things in life delight me. I rejoice in textures, in smells, in sights and storms and childhood memories. I have found that when the power in these things breaks over me anew, the best response is to worship—for truly, it is the imagination and power of the Creator I delight in. As a woman who praises the painter or musician who has moved her, so I worship my God, who has enriched my heart with His painting; with His story; with His song.

You are home, my home, my God.

You are my window from which to watch the rain and hear it beat its unfailing time. You are the wood beneath my feet when I watch the lightning and I hear the thunder.

You are the trees that grow and live and comfort with their unchanging presence.

You are glittering white stones in the driveway and weeds that grow up through cracks in the walk. You are split-rail fences and barns with haylofts; You are birds chirping and apples growing and the seasons turning; summer and winter, seedtime and harvest; always and ever and on.

You are snow angels and Christmas lights and blizzards and grey skies and deep winter silence.

You are home, my home, my God!

You are children laughing and the old ones smiling and the peaceful love of family. You are that which does not change, the home in which I am a child again, and there are no fears You do not have the power to calm.

On You I sleep, and eat; run and laugh; hide and dream and play.

Home, my home, my God!

Second Thoughts

"After this manner therefore pray ye: Our Father, which art in heaven..."[1]

The second line of the Lord's Prayer always seemed a little superfluous to me. God is God. Of course He's in heaven. Another thing: when I first began to study the prayer, I didn't like that line much. I wanted God to be on Earth, where I assumed He was better able to hear and help me. And of course, He is on earth. He is everywhere, a mystery which my little sisters and brothers can discuss for hours ("is God in that chair? is He in the toothpaste tube?"). God is in Heaven, and He is on Earth.

So why "our Father, which art in heaven"? Why did Jesus take the time to include these words in this prayer of all prayers?

First of all, to say that God is in Heaven is to say that He is above. This is important. He is above my problems; He is "the rock that is higher than I." By this I do not mean that He is far away or uncaring. I mean that He is above life's difficulties; therefore He is not tangled up in them. I sink in the storm, He walks on the water. I am a ground squirrel, running here and there, ears perked up for danger but unable to comprehend that which is more than a few feet away. He is the eagle, soaring high above, whose eyes see and un-

1   Matthew 6:9

derstand the whole where I can only see a small part. Now and then He comes down and covers me with His feathers. I nestle under the shadow of His wings and sleep in peace, content to trust Him, because He is above me.

I've decided that I very much like having a God who is not tied down by gravity; a God who can't be confused or shaken or fooled. My rock, my fortress, my high tower—my Father in Heaven.

A Samuel Generation

He was born as an answer to his mother's prayer; dedicated to God before he could walk. He was raised by the High Priest of Israel and grew to be a man of God, of whom it was said that God "let none of his words fall to the ground."[1] He was a prophet and the last judge of Israel: the one who made the way for the king, who anointed David to sit on the throne of Jerusalem.

His name was Samuel. Sometimes I think he and I have a lot in common.

You, too. Do you doubt it? You were born again in answer to someone's prayer. God chose you for Himself before you could walk. Chances are you've spent a lot of time in the Temple—in church culture, singing in the choir, memorizing your verses; listening to the sermon, maybe even preaching it. Your service has been sincere and real and God has accepted it. As to Samuel's unique place in history, as the man who stood in the gap between two eras—well, who can say what will come after us? We may be in the last days. We too prepare the way for our King.

But there's something in Samuel's story I'd like to

---

1   I Samuel 3:19

point out: when God called him, in I Samuel 3:4, the boy who had served the Lord all his life did not recognize His voice. Does this mean that all of Samuel's years of service prior to this had been a sham, a series of empty, wasted years? No. He spent those years serving God, and God spent them preparing him to enter a whole new era in his spiritual life.

All the Sunday school lessons, principles, "right-thinking," good practices, Bible study, and seminary lessons in the world can never measure up to a single encounter with the living God. The one who sees God is forever changed.

Samuel's call was not the end of his walk in the supernatural. I Samuel 3:21 records that "the Lord appeared again in Shiloh: for the Lord revealed himself to Samuel by the word of the Lord."

When I was fourteen, I had an experience similar to Samuel's. I was born into a Christian family with generations of believers on both sides. I grew up in church. Moreover, I was always inclined to take spiritual things seriously. As a nine-year-old I did my best to evangelize the neighbours. I tried to make myself cry over the crucifixion. I rededicated my life umpteen times throughout my childhood and early teens. I ruled in Bible trivia.

My family moved out to California and I found myself looked up to in youth group because I was so spiritual. I knew all the right answers; I tried to be obedient and live a godly life. But inside I was starving. Call me a melodramatic teenager (and I probably was), but I remember going to God in desperation one day and telling Him that if this was all there was, I was through. It was time to go my own way. As far as I could see, I had reached the limits of what Christianity had to offer—and it wasn't enough.

That same week I huddled in a dark room and listened to party-goers celebrating the New Year outside my window. I felt desperately alone. I thought I could understand why some people consider suicide—it hurt so much to live. Two words passed through my mind, frozen in empty significance: "You're alone."

And on the heels of that thought the Hound of Heaven came howling in. "You're not," said a new voice. "The Holy Spirit is here."

I can't explain what happened at that room in that moment. Amy Carmichael once described a similar experience by saying that "the darkness became light around me." I knew God was there. I could almost touch Him. The air that I breathed was joy and peace. I fell asleep in absolute peace, knowing with all my heart that He loved me and was with me.

Did that "spiritual high" last? Of course not. But I had been changed. In the next year, God began to open the floodgates and show me who He was. Scripture blazed to life. Praise songs burst into glory. Even the dust beneath my feet caused me to rejoice, because He had once walked on dust just like it! Today, the echoes of that time still shape my life. I cannot always feel God. Sometimes I doubt His word. But I know that I know that I know He is real—and I know that He is love. I know. I've been with Him.

Before Samuel was called, God told the High Priest Eli that "I will raise me up a faithful priest, that shall do according to that which is in mine heart and in my mind."[1] This is what I believe God wants to do in our

---
1 I Samuel 2:35

lives. He is not looking for a group of people to keep a list of rules or agree with a set of propositions. He is looking for a people who will seek Him, who will love Him, who will know Him so well that they can do according to all that is in God's heart and in His mind! It is true, we can never achieve this on our own. No amount of prayer, praise, or service will reveal God to us. He can only reveal Himself. But I believe that He wants to do so—and that He will.

God is not interested in setting us on spiritual mountaintops for all time. He wants us to know the depths of who He is, and so we must go through deep places in our lives. Suffering and abundance, sorrow and joy, heartache and a cup that runneth over—all serve to reveal Him. We must open our eyes; we must look for Him, because He is looking for us. His first purpose is not to make us happy. His first purpose is to reveal Himself to us, and in so doing, to make us like Him.

The New Testament resounds with this great anthem. Jesus came to reveal the Father. The Holy Spirit comes to reveal Jesus. Paul's letters sing with the joy of one to whom the Lord had appeared. The writer of Hebrews urges us to "leave the principles of the doctrine of Christ and go on unto perfection,"[1] to follow Jesus beyond the veil into the Holy of Holies, into the very presence of the Living God.

Thousands of years ago David, the psalmist and king, cried out to God to come and fulfill all of his deepest longings. "O God, thou art my God," he said: "Early will I seek thee: my soul thirsteth for thee, my flesh longeth for thee in a dry and thirsty land, where no water is; To see thy power and thy glory, so as I have

---

1   Hebrews 6:1, 19-20

seen thee in the sanctuary."[1]

My friends, my family, know that God has called you to this. "This is life eternal," Jesus said in John 17:3, "that they might know thee the only true God, and Jesus Christ whom thou hast sent."

---

[1] Psalm 63:1-2

Kingdoms of Light...

"To look up into a dark sky and see it suddenly open as lightning plays across it, to see in one revealing flash deep into the kingdoms of light, is to know what prayer most truly is. There is mystery, but beyond that darkness is not a deeper darkness, but light—kingdoms of light."

Amy Carmichael, from *Ploughed Under*

notes from the author

These past few months have been times of intense prayer for me: on my own behalf, yes, but more intensely on the behalf of others. Sometimes it seems as though everything is going wrong, and we Christians are "the great company of the brokenhearted," limping along together. Together we refuse to let circumstances overwhelm us. Together we trust in God in the face of all the Enemy can do. My friends, I stand with you.

In the Morning

One of these years I plan to start a new tradition. Every year in February or March—shortly before the visible coming of spring, while the world is still cold and grey—I'll go out early in the morning, light a bonfire, worship my God, and wait for the sun to rise. The purpose? By faith to welcome in the spring, celebrate morning, and look to the rising of the Sun of Righteousness.

When we first turn our hearts over to God, the whole world seems to bloom into summer. Pastures are green; sparkling rivers of water are ever there to slake our thirst. The Shepherd walks where we can see Him and often smiles down on us. The sunlight is gentle and heartening. It's hard to believe that winter will ever come again.

But it does. Every high mountain path leads again into the valleys. As in the far north, months pass in which the sun does not rise. The rivers freeze over, and the blowing snow obscures our vision of the One we follow—even His footprints disappear.

When the sun is long in coming and warmth is a waning memory, when we can see our way to the cross but not beyond it—what then are we, the children of God, to do?

Hold on to hope. David said it best when he called us to sing out of the darkness: "Sing unto the Lord, O ye saints of his, and give thanks at the remembrance of his holiness. For his anger endureth but a moment: in his favour is life: weeping may endure for a night, but joy cometh in the morning."[1]

Believe. In John 9, Jesus healed a man blind from the day he was born. That man, enshrouded in darkness from the moment of birth, could not imagine what it was like to see. It wasn't his ability to envision healing that caused him to be healed, but the compassion and holiness of Jesus! You needn't work yourself into a special state of mind, what we sometimes call "faith," to be healed. You need only have faith in God—in who He is. Your testimony and mine will one day echo the blind man's: "One thing I know, that, whereas I was blind, now I see."

Spring is coming. The sun will rise. The darkness cannot last forever.

Rejoice. "My brethren," says James, "count it all joy when ye fall into divers temptations."[2] This concept doesn't belong only to the New Testament. Lovers of God have always known that rejoicing was an appropriate response to hardship. As David said, when everything seems darkest, sing unto the Lord and give thanks at the remembrance of His holiness. So the world has fallen down around you—your life isn't anchored in the world. It never was. God is still there, God is still holy and good; so rejoice! You will overcome.

St. John of the Cross once said, "One act of thanksgiving made when things go wrong is worth a thousand when things go well." Why? When we thank God in darkness, we proclaim that we are too small to see

1   Psalm 30:5
2   James 1:2

what is truly happening. The Only-Wise God is still in control, and He has promised to work everything out to our good. When everything spins out of control, we must surrender our definitions of "wrong" and "well" and let God work His greater purpose in and through us.

Trust Him. Trust the Father as Jesus did in Gethsemane; as Paul and Silas did when their praises rocked their prison; as Daniel did from the lion's den. God took each to the brink of death before He delivered them—in one case, He took Him beyond it. The history of God's people rings with the voices of those who trusted in darkness: Jeanne Guyon, who compared herself to a bird singing praises to God from the "cage" of the Bastille; Jim Elliot, whose death in Ecuador at a young age inspired hundreds to go the mission field he so loved; Corrie ten Boom, who discovered that the light of God could still shine in the darkness of a Nazi death camp. This is the cloud of witnesses that surround us, therefore,

"Let us lay aside every weight, and the sin which doth so easily beset us, and let us run with patience the race that is set before us, Looking unto Jesus the author and finisher of our faith; who for the joy that was set before him endured the cross, despising the shame, and is set down at the right hand of God."[1]

Suffering is not a strange thing in the Christian life. Jesus Himself did not escape it, nor did He try. Glory only comes after trials; spring never comes without a winter before it. Endure the cross, for it leads to joy. Look unto Jesus, remember His holiness, sing and praise Him. Trust.

The morning will come.

---

1 Hebrews 12:1-2

Credo

I believe in the sun even when it is not shining.
I believe in love even when feeling it not.
I believe in God even when He is silent.
Hear my prayer, hear my prayer,
I believe,
I believe.

> Graffiti on the walls of a cellar in Germany
> where Jews hid from the Nazis.

notes from the author

Seven years ago, in California, my parents, sisters, brothers, and I dug all of the internationally-styled clothing we could find out of our closets and dressed up to reflect our European heritage. We were going to a celebration, the theme of which was "Gathering of the Nations." When we arrived, the array of colours (in skin and clothing, not to mention in personality) was stunning. We were greeted by young women in moosehide dresses and fur-lined mukluks, regal Africans in long, colourful robes and turbans, Asians in traditional dress, even by a missionary friend in a bewildering combination of scarves, polka-dots, stripes, and layers that was said to be typical of Russian peasantry. We had gathered to celebrate the multi-decade anniversary of a missionary enterprise that had impacted all of our lives. More truly, we had gathered to celebrate the work done in us by the Son of God.

The night was free and beautiful as we worshiped together, riding on waves of joy that filled the room. Midway through the evening, a tall black woman stepped up to the mic and led us in a call-and-response song from Nigeria. She began with the question, "What manner of man is Jesus?" and the congregation answered with a harmonic "Hallelujah!" Each verse began with the same question, and ended as she extolled His actions, His character, His holiness. Much of the song was made up on the spot. Always the response was the same: "Hallelujah."

The question is at the heart of all that Christians believe, and it must be at the core of our lives. "What manner of man is Jesus?"

The Holy Mystery
WHAT MANNER OF MAN IS JESUS: PART I

Sweet little Jesus boy
They made you be born in a manger.
Sweet little Holy Child
We didn't know who you were

Before the beginning, there was God. A great Being characterized by love, joy, holiness, and creative power. From His beautiful mind the world was created, and in it were placed the man and his wife, created to walk with God.

Things changed. Man exercised his power of choice and drove a wedge between the Creator and the created, for the One was holy, and the other a walking death. For thousands of years God spoke into the world from a distance. He inspired the writings we now call "the Bible." He covered Himself in fire and darkness and descended on Mt. Sinai. He sent angels. He gave visions.

And then He came.

The Hebrew prophet Isaiah spoke of the Coming: "Therefore the Lord himself shall give you a sign; Behold, a virgin shall conceive, and bear a son, and shall call his name Immanuel."[1] Immanuel. It means "God with us."

God came. He wrapped bright spirit in human flesh and filled human veins with Life, and the one we call the Son of God was born into the world. They named Him Jesus, for it was said that He would save His people from their sins. A 5th century hymn imagines the scene from a heavenly perspective:

> *Rank on rank the host of heaven*
> *Spreads its vanguard on the way*
> *As the Light of light descendeth*
> *From the realms of endless day*
> *That the powers of hell may vanish*
> *As the darkness clears away.*

As often as we talk about the Incarnation—every year at Christmas, each time we quote John 3:16—I think we forget. Our world trivializes everything, and unfortunately the Church has followed suit in many ways. We can turn on Christian radio and listen to Scooby-Doo singing "Hallelujah"; we can turn on secular television Christmas morning and watch a lonely cartoon Jesus sing "Happy Birthday to Me" on South Park. Wonder goes by the wayside as the profane swallows the sacred, and we forget.

Will you allow me to remind you?

The Son lived long before we had a name for Him. He lived in the Time Before Time. Creation, in particular humanity, is filled with evidence of Him. If man was made in the image of the Father, then every child

---

[1] Isaiah 7:14

is made in the image of the Son. What we call "family" existed first in the love of the Father and the Son for each other. Marriage too is a reflection of His love for humanity, for He declared Himself to be the Eternal Bridegroom seeking a bride.

He is the source of life, this precious thing we all have inside of us. Scientists searching for the origins of life will never find it in a primordial soup, for it comes straight from the Being whose existence they deny. The Apostle John tells us that "All things were made by him, and without him was not any thing made that was made. In him was life; and the life was the light of men."[1]

He is the One we long for. Have you ever wondered why so many of the people who followed Jesus were in such a sinful mess when He came? The prostitutes and tax collectors Jesus is famous for reaching weren't even trying to live good lives until they caught sight of His holiness. They were driven by hunger. Every choice they made was a grasping for something to fill their emptiness, and when He came to them, at last they found the only one who could satisfy. Jesus declared Himself to be the Bread of God, the Water of Life, the Way we must follow, the Treasure we greatly desire. Human beings are full of hunger, and though we so often chase sinful things in an effort to fill it, ultimately we are hungry because we need Jesus Christ. He is at the bottom of every longing. He made us for Himself.

All of this was formed in human flesh, made to find sustenance in a young girl's womb. Jesus was a man, yes. He was fully man, and He means for us to relate to Him as a man. But was immeasurably more, and we

1   John 1:3-4

cannot allow ourselves to forget that. The Shining Man who Peter saw on the Mount of Transfiguration wasn't a "new" Jesus—He was the Jesus who had always been, the Ancient of Days in human flesh.

This should make a difference to the way we live our lives. It should affect the way we pray, because we're not asking things in the name of the Nice Joe down the street; we're asking in the Name of Jesus. It should affect the way we look at the world around us, because Creation still bears testimony to His eternal existence. Most of all, it should affect the way we view our relationship with God. You see, through Jesus, God has defined our relationship with Him in many human terms. He calls us "child," "brother, sister, mother," "servant," "friend." As I muse over these things, I am overcome with the knowledge that the Ever-Existent One, the Eternal Son of the Father, has reached out to me. We are called to a relationship with God.

> *At His feet the six-winged seraph,*
> *Cherubim, with sleepless eye,*
> *Veil their faces in His presence*
> *As with ceaseless voice they cry:*
> *Alleluia! Alleluia!*
> *Alleluia! Lord Most High!*

The song quotes are from "Sweet Little Jesus Boy" by Robert MacGimsey and "The Liturgy of St. James."

A Great Light
WHAT MANNER OF MAN IS JESUS: PART II

"And they shall look unto the earth; and behold trouble and darkness, dimness of anguish; and they shall be driven to darkness."

Thousands of years ago, the prophet Isaiah spoke of a time when darkness would overwhelm the earth. But in the midst of this great darkness, God would birth a new and wondrous thing: "The people that walked in darkness have seen a great light: they that dwell in the land of the shadow of death, upon them hath the light shined."[1]

Isaiah's prophecy was fulfilled in a very unexpected way. The Light came with a name, with a body that lived perfection and a tongue that set the world blazing. His name was Jesus.

Years after Jesus' time on Earth had ended, the apostle John summed up what he had learned through Him: "This then is the message which we have heard of him, and declare unto you, that God is light, and in him is no darkness at all."[2] Throughout history God has revealed Himself to man. Through the Law, where we first learned that God has absolute standards of <u>righteousness</u>. Through His power, in His miracles

---

1   Isaiah 8:22-9:2
2   I John 1:5

and multiple deliverances of Israel. Through poetry, prophecy, and allegory, as He poured out His desires and demands through the prophets. But not until the Son of God came to Earth did light truly shine in our darkness. Not until we watched Him live did we finally come to understand the heart of God.

Recently I was talking with a fellow Christian who told me that he's had trouble understanding the God of the New Testament. It's hard to grasp the Almighty as Jesus presented Him, he said. My friend found it much easier to connect to the Old Testament: to the prophets and commandments, miracles and laws. I understood, because up until recently I've found the four Gospels to be the hardest books in the Bible to understand. Yet, if I believe what scripture tells me, I realize that I cannot know God until I know Him in Jesus Christ. Until the Son opens my eyes, I will always misunderstand the Father.

If the Church today needs anything, it needs a clearer vision of Jesus. Paul calls Him "the visible image of the invisible God."[1] Jesus Himself declared that no man comes to the Father except through Him.[2] What manner of man is Jesus? If we want to know God, it is imperative that we find out. We've got to come to Him, impoverished in spirit, hungering and thirsting for righteousness, with no pretense and no religious games. Jesus was never impressed with those who pretended righteousness in a bid to win God's favour. God does not require us to get it together before we come, He just says Come. He'll take care of the rest.

I'm a needy person. There's a lot of emptiness in me, a lot of darkness. And rather than attempt to chase

---

1 (Colossians 1:15, NLT)
2 (John 14:6)

out the darkness, I need to let in the light. I go to scripture desperate these days. I call on the Holy Spirit to open my eyes every time I open the Book. I want to see Jesus, and I can't do that through my own power. I can read about Him; I can memorize His teachings. But Christ wasn't just a conduit for a message. He was a Man, the Son of God. It's His essence, His life, that I need. John speaks to me once again when he calls Jesus "that eternal life, which was with the Father, and was manifested to us."[1] We've seen Jesus, John says; we've seen the life. Light has come.

In the Church we talk about strategies and paradigms and movements. We follow prophets and pastors and people who can play the guitar. We draw lines and form clubs and quibble over words, and often we do it with a sincere heart. We're trying to figure out how to do our religion right. But we've got to remember that we're not followers of a creed, a religion, or a message; we're disciples of a man. We get off track when we lose sight of that. People of God, we need to follow Him.

There has never been a man like Jesus, never a leader so worthy to be followed. Early in Jesus' ministry, Matthew records that "the people were astonished at his doctrine: For he taught them as one having authority, and not as the scribes."[2] As no other man in history, Jesus practiced what He preached. He had the authority of a pure life. We can see His commandments as unfair and kick against them, until we remember that He never asked us for anything that He didn't give first. He asked them to throw away earthly treasures and securities and follow Him, after He had given up heaven

---

1 I John 1:2
2 Matthew 7:28-19

for their sakes. He called for purity and holiness, and He alone never gave in to temptation. He told them to take up their crosses, but He was the first to be crucified.

In a dark world, Jesus shone as a light. He still does. There is nothing more powerfully attractive than a person, a word, an action through which Jesus lives. "*WWJD?*" is more than a question to wear around your wrist: it's a call to search out the heart of God. Don't try to keep Jesus' commandments because your striving will earn you favour. It won't. But an attempt to walk as He walked may open new doors to knowing Him, and move us closer to the goal of Creation: "Whoso keepeth his word, in him verily is the love of God perfected."[1] Jesus alone can bring us to the Father. Jesus alone can open our eyes. Jesus alone can teach us to love.

People of God, we need to know Him.

He has chosen us, saved us, loved us to the grave and back again. He calls us to holiness and raises a higher standard than the Law ever did. The first of His commandments is "Love God," and not one of us has ever truly loved an abstraction. To use a phrase that's been hollowed out and stereotyped over the years, we need a relationship with Jesus. Many years after Jesus' death, in the twilight of the twelve apostles' lives, John declared that he and the early Christians were still walking with their Risen Lord. "That which we have seen and heard declare we unto you, that ye also may have fellowship with us: and truly our fellowship is with the Father, and with his Son Jesus Christ."[2]

---

1 I John 2:5
2 I John 1:3

Did You Enjoy This Book?

Do you know someone who would benefit by reading it? SPREAD THE WORD! As a small press, we value the power of READERS to decide what is worth reading. We believe that a book's true value cannot be measured in marketing dollars. The worth of a book is in the impact it has on YOUR life. If you have seen value in this book, we encourage you to let others know.

IT'S SIMPLE:
- Spread the word!
- Give a copy as a gift.
- Leave a review at your favourite online retailer (Amazon, Barnes & Noble, etc).
- If you write a newsletter, ezine, blog, or print column, consider letting your readers know about this book!
- Send us an e-mail to let us know how much this book has touched you: publisher@littledozen.com

VISIT

www.littledozen.com

FOR
Inspirational Books
Bible Studies
Novels
Short Stories
Articles
Order Information & Bulk Discounts

Visit Rachel Starr Thomson
www.rachelstarrthomson.com

Heart to Heart: Meeting With God in the Lord's Prayer

Chapter 1: Our Father

*After this manner therefore
pray ye: Our Father...*

ONCE, A VERY LONG TIME AGO, THERE WAS A GARDEN. Six days of uproarious joy created it. Out of darkness came a Voice, and then light, galaxies spinning, earth and water, wings and running feet—life. There was nothing, and then there was colour: green trees, blue seas, shimmering grey mists. And a garden.

Then the One to whom the Voice belonged stooped down and made something with His hands. He "formed man of the dust of the ground, and breathed into his nostrils the breath of life; and man became a living soul."[1]

There was life before Adam, but the dust-man had something the other living creatures did not have. He

---

1   Genesis 2:7

was a living soul. Somehow his existence, his being, reflected the Being of his Creator. The Living God and the Living Soul fellowshipped together in the garden. They walked together in the cool of the day. Their relationship was the heartbeat of Eden.

I wonder what Adam called God. When he opened his eyes and knew that the Creator was, what did he call him?

Names play a big part in the Genesis story. God named Adam. Adam named Eve and all the animals. Names are important because they put us into relationship with those around us. I dislike name tags, because I think if someone wants to know my name he ought to take the trouble to ask for it, and so create a relationship between us. What I call someone—mother, father, judge, officer, first name, pet name—determines who he is to me and who I am to him.

We don't know what Adam called God. That is because the day came when the heartbeat of Eden stopped, when the relationship was severed, and Adam, once called a Living Soul, began to die.

Generations later, people had not only forgotten God's name. By and large, they had forgotten He even existed.

"Now the Lord said unto Abram, Get thee out of thy country, and from thy kindred, and from thy father's house unto a land that I will shew thee: And I will make of thee a great nation, and I will bless thee, and make thy name great; and thou shalt be a blessing: And I will bless them that bless thee, and curse him that curseth thee: and in thee shall all families of the earth be blessed."[1]

And so a new chapter began. God began the process that would one day restore Eden.

Abram called God "Lord." It sounds natural to us, but it didn't to Abram's contemporaries. "Lord." Lord of what? The nations of the world had lords for everything. One lord for the Nile, one lord for the farm, one lord for the city, one lord for the house; lords and gods galore. Their gods all had names to connect them to their specific role, their specific place of lordship. And here were Abram and his descendants running around referring to "Lord" and "God."

Four hundred years after Abram had become Abraham—"Father of Many"—one of the Many approached a burning bush and saw God there. In that moment something in him reached out to know who this God of Abraham was.

"And Moses said unto God, Behold, when I come unto the children of Israel, and shall say unto them, The God of your fathers hath sent me unto you; and they shall say to me, What is his name? What shall I say unto them? And God said unto Moses, I Am That I Am: and he said, Thus shalt thou say unto the children of Israel, I Am hath sent me unto you."[2]

If Moses had hoped to pin God down and put Him in a glass case with a neat label underneath, his hopes were shattered. "I Am That I Am." Such a name takes God outside of this world's limitations, outside of our whole sphere of reference. Only the Creator, the Voice from the garden, could possess such a name.

The name given to Moses is often translated as

---
1 Genesis 12:1-3
2 Exodus 3:13-14

"Yahweh" or "Jehovah." Throughout the Old Testament, it is indicated by spelling "Lord" in capital letters. He is the awe-inspiring Adoshem, "Lord of the Name." Because they do not wish to take the name of the Lord in vain, Orthodox Jews often refer to God simply as Hashem—"The Name."

∽

A cluster of men sat around their leader, a man with rough hands and an unsophisticated northern accent. "Lord," they asked, "teach us to pray."

And He said, "After this manner pray ye: Our Father which art in heaven..."[1]

Jesus of Nazareth had a way of using unexpected words to turn a discussion of the ordinary on its head. For example: "Father."

He called Hashem "Father."

Our Father.

With one word, the carpenter placed us into a new relationship with God. Not the relationship of subject to king, of prisoner to judge, or even of dust to Creator. He put us into the relationship of child to father.

This changes everything.

I pray, "Give me bread." And I need not come with my head bowed to the dirt, groveling, begging. I need not come with something to trade, some price to pay that I may eat. God is my Father, and "what man is there of you, whom if his son ask bread, will he give him a stone? Or if he ask a fish, will he give him a serpent? If ye then, being evil, know how to give good gifts unto your children, how much more shall your

---
1   Matthew 6:9

Father which is in heaven give good things to them that ask him?"[1]

I pray, "Forgive my debts." And though I come smelling like pigs and filthy from time spent wallowing in the world's muck, I do not ask forgiveness of a judge who sits high above me in anger and malice. I ask it of a father who is watching for me, as Jesus said in the story of the Prodigal Son: "But when he was yet a great way off, his father saw him, and had compassion, and ran, and fell on his neck, and kissed him."[2]

Welcome, child. Welcome to the garden.

"Thy kingdom come." Revive the heartbeat. Walk with God again.

For nearly two years when I was a teenager, my parents went away almost every weekend to work at trade shows, while I stayed home and babysat the youngest six children. We had a perfectly nice time at home without them. But when I would go to bed at night, I was never entirely at peace. No matter how well I handled the household or how much fun we had, I could not truly breathe easily until they were home again.

Even so, we do not have peace until Abba comes home.

Jesus rarely used any word but "Father" to describe God. Well; and He had the right. He is the only begotten Son of God, is He not? As I write this, I have a disquieted feeling that I may be on dangerous ground. God is a judge, a king, a Creator. I don't wish to encourage irreverence for Him. Maybe I am wrong to say that He is our loving Father.

Maybe there is a Father, there is a Son, and there are

---

[1] Matthew 7:9-11
[2] Luke 15:20

millions of little minions (us).

The truth is, I can hardly believe it myself. I am still trying that word on for size: "Father." Our Father.

∞

Once—also a long time ago, but not so long as before—there was another garden. A woman stood in it, weeping. She had loved a man and placed all of her hope in him, and he was dead. Now his body had been stolen and every last shred of dignity denied him.

"Woman," a voice said, "why weepest thou?"

She turned, and through her tears saw a man approaching. A gardener, in all probability.

"Sir," she said, "if thou hast borne him hence, tell me where thou hast laid him, and I will take him away."

(Dear Mary Magdalene—if she could have lifted Jesus' broken body alone and carried Him away somewhere safe, I think she would have done it.)

He said, "Mary."

And she knew.

"Rabboni," she cried, "Master."

"Jesus saith unto her, Touch me not; for I am not yet ascended to my Father: but go to my brethren, and say unto them, I ascend unto my Father, and your Father; and to my God, and your God."[1]

∞

"But when ye pray, use not vain repetitions, as the heathen do: for they think that they shall be heard for their much speaking. Be not ye therefore like unto them: for your Father knoweth what things ye have

---

[1] John 20:14-17

need of, before ye ask him. After this manner therefore pray ye:

"Our Father, which art in heaven..."

Welcome, child, to the garden.

Thy kingdom come.

**Heart to Heart:
Meeting With God in the Lord's Prayer**

is available for purchase at www.LittleDozen.com, from multiple online retailers, or special order from your local bookstore.

www.ingramcontent.com/pod-product-compliance
Lightning Source LLC
Chambersburg PA
CBHW030319080526
44584CB00012B/622